1982

NOMADS, EXILES, & EMIGRES

The Rebirth of the Latin American Narrative, 1960-80

Ronald Schwartz

The Scarecrow Press, Inc.
Metuchen, N.J., & London, 1980

Library of Congress Cataloging in Publication Data

Schwartz, Ronald, 1937-
   Nomads, exiles, and emigres.

   Bibliography: p.
   Includes index.
   1. Spanish American fiction--20th century--
History and criticism. I. Title.
PQ7082.N7S39   863'.009'98   80-20669
ISBN 0-8108-1359-9

In memory of Arthur E. Fletcher

ACKNOWLEDGMENTS

Many people are responsible for the arousal of my interest in Latin America and its literature, notably Robert G. Mead, who first awakened my consciousness to Mexico and the splendors of Carlos Fuentes's first novel in 1958. However, my interest was nourished principally through travel and the acquaintance with many Latin American scholars, novelists, critics, translators, teachers, and friends. I would like to thank particularly Thomas Colchie, Gregory Kolovakos, Carlos Fuentes, Emir Rodríguez Monegal, and Manuel Puig for their inspiration, as well as John Brushwood, Seymour Menton, Harvey Oberhelman, Gregory Rabassa, and Kessel Schwartz for many thoughts that have found their way into the composition of this book.

Of course I am grateful to the librarians I have worked with at City University, particularly Florence Hauser, Sharad Karkhanis, Adele Schneider, Angelo Tripicchio, and their chairperson, John Clune, for helping me to secure materials, and to my own chairperson, Julio Hernández-Miyares, for his enthusiastic interest and help especially pertaining to contemporary Cuban novelists.

I also wish to thank the following for permission to reprint material appearing in this volume: Georges Borchardt, Inc. , and Dutton for Severo Sarduy's Cobra; Harper & Row for Guillermo Cabrera Infante's View of Dawn in the Tropics, Gabriel García Márquez's The Autumn of the Patriarch and Mario Vargas Llosa's Sergeant Pantoja and the Special Service; Harold Matson Co. , Inc. , for Explosion in a Cathedral, Copyright © 1962 by Alejo Carpentier; and Random House, Inc. , and Alfred A. Knopf, Inc. , for Manuel Puig's Kiss of the Spiderwoman, translated by Thomas Colchie, and for critical material by Emir

Rodríguez Monegal from The Borzoi Anthology of Latin American Literature, Volume II.

A note of appreciation to my "Texas" friend and colleague Dr. Allen Richman at Stephen Austin State College in Nacogdoches, whose interest, encouragement, and affection has sustained me throughout the years.

Finally, I am grateful for the patience of my wife, Amelia, and son, Jonathan Fletcher, during the writing of this volume and to Norma Shear at Scarecrow Press. (And a special thank you to Arnie and Jack at Zeimar for their good cheer at lunchtime during the composition of Nomads.)

Ronald Schwartz
City University of New York

TABLE OF CONTENTS

PREFACE

This book is a modest attempt to popularize the "new" Latin American novel in the United States for readers of English. It is offered as a critical work for those with little or no knowledge of Spanish. I will examine ten major authors active during the last twenty years whose novels have been translated into English, reviewing and analyzing at least one major work of each writer in depth. Some of these novels have already been declared "landmarks" by many astute critics of Latin American fiction and have achieved the distinction of translation into English. My goal is to point out the literary and entertainment values of these novels, elevate the American reader's consciousness, and proselytize on behalf of writers who are finally achieving their long-deserved success among their international competitors.

One last note: the selection of novels by a particular author is mine alone; in some cases I have chosen to analyze books that have not yet achieved "landmark" status simply because of underexposure to critical analysis, but these are equally worthy of their authors and are accessible in English translation.

INTRODUCTION

There is no easy way to summarize the development of the Latin American novel through 1960. However, by virtue of their birth dates the authors discussed in this book all belong to a particular literary generation characterized by a prevailing artistic ideology. Carpentier (1904) clearly belongs to the generation of 1927, when surrealism was the prevailing artistic mode of expression. Lezama Lima (1912) and Cortázar (1914) are placed in the generation of 1942, when neorealism or the revival of nineteenth-century realism was in vogue. Donoso (1924), García Márquez (1928), Fuentes (1929), Cabrera Infante (1929), and Puig (1933) belong to the generation of 1957, when writers and artists concentrated on fantasy, the grotesque, the strange and experimental, the irrational and unreal, in their works. Vargas Llosa (1936) and Sarduy (1937) belong to the generation of 1972, writers who resist classification, the newest of the experimentalists, who utilize shifts in time and space, dramatic counterpoint, and abrupt stylistic changes in their portrayals of diverse and never-before-treated sectors of Latin American society. It is clear the Latin American novel has undergone the most radical artistic changes since the 1920s, and the period 1960-80 represents a true synthesis of polarities of style within the four generations of writers previously cited.

The period 1960-80, representing the renascence of the Latin American narrative, was chosen for reasons other than literary and stylistic. The political and social fabric of Latin America had been in flux since pre-Colombian times, but never was the "boom" in Latin American fiction more attributable to the politics over the past twenty-five years. For example, the overthrow of the Batista dictatorship by Fidel Castro in Cuba in 1956 and the resulting "boom" of the

Cuban narrative in the early 1960s points up a correlation
between the creative output of Cuban nomads, exiles, and
émigrés and their society. Almost all the writers during
this period were displaced from their homeland, some never
to return: hence, their status as nomads, exiles, and émigrés, creative novelists probing the fabric of their societies
during a period of war, dictatorships, and coups d'état. The
demise of Trujillo's dictatorship of Santo Domingo in 1961,
Perón's of Argentina in 1955 and 1973, and the military overthrow of Allende's Marxist government in Chile also in 1973
certainly affected the intellectual atmosphere for many Latin
American writers. Just as the Munich massacre of athletes
was world-shattering, so was the 1968 Olympic Games in
Mexico City notable because of student riots. The Vietnam
War also contributed greatly to the uneasy international situation between the United States and Latin America. Assuredly,
many of the writers treated in this volume may appear somewhat desafinado, or out of tune with world history, but their
collective social consciousness appears to have become
alerted and distilled over the past twenty years, judging by
the breadth and depth of their fictions, especially during
these "boom" years.

Another factor contributing to the renascence of the
Latin American novel is the phenomenon known as the "boom"
or the great flash of interest in Latin American writers and
publications in the early 1960s. The concept of the "boom"
was probably a promotional stunt by Latin American publishers to promote the serious works of many of the younger
nomads, exiles, and émigrés, who suddenly became visible
and marketable commodities, readily available in English
translation in the United States. The "boom" phenomenon
was amply abetted by a proliferation of hastily translated
novels, poetry, and criticism, materials that identified the
"new" Latin American narrative's propensity for new narrative techniques, innovative language, and cosmopolitan and
universal themes. What emerged was a group of writers
searching for their roots, their national identities, exploring
the social and moral issues of the continent in their works.
It has been suggested that certain "boom" authors have col-
laborated with American critics and publishers for mutual
cultural and financial gain, that the "boom" was a manufac-
tured phenomenon and not the spontaneous literary movement
as it had originally evolved. Nevertheless, the "boom" has
benefitted the flourishing of interest in Latin American literature, history, and bibliography, and several of the writers
under consideration in this volume owe their careers to the

blaze of the "boom" phenomenon.   At this point, let us discover the writers and their novels and the reasons Latin
American fiction has finally attained its long-deserved international stature.

1. CARPENTIER: CUBAN COSMOPOLITE, BAROQUE STYLIST

Considered by most critics the single most productive Latin American writer, Alejo Carpentier has contributed a steady stream of fiction from the early 1930s up to the present moment, irrespective of the various "booms" or highlights taking place in South America and elsewhere over the past twenty years. Carpentier, with a very fine international reputation as a novelist, remains one of those Latin American writers who is consistently translated into English. Explosion in a Cathedral, his major novel and the third to be translated into English, is written in the frame of a traditional realist novel.

Born in Havana, Cuba, on December 26, 1904, of mixed French and Russian parentage,[1] Carpentier has had a multifaceted career. Besides writing novels, he is also a renowned journalist and musicologist. His father emigrated to Cuba in 1902 and endowed him with a cosmopolitan and skeptical upbringing. After attending Candler College and the Colegio Mimo, he studied music and architecture at the University of Havana. He began writing prose in his early teens while cultivating a musical talent, a lyrical element always present in his later fiction. In the early 1920s he abandoned his university studies and began a career as a commercial journalist, becoming editor-in-chief of Carteles, a literary magazine. Traveling frequently to Mexico in the late twenties, he was jailed on his return to Cuba in 1927 after signing a manifesto against the dictator Machado. Eventually released after spending forty days in jail, he traveled to Paris in 1928 with the aid of surrealist poet Robert Desnos. It was in Paris of the late twenties that Carpentier rediscovered Latin America. The eleven years

1

he spent abroad were essential to his artistic formation. Although he began his first novel in Cuba, Ecué-yamba-o, an exercise in nativistic folklore patterns, Carpentier plunged into the Parisian surrealist mode, taking up with André Bretón, Louis Aragon, and Tristan Tzara among others. Although his sympathy with the surrealist movement was shortlived, it did show him how to view aspects of American life that he had not seen before. Guiraldes, Gallegos, and Riviera were influential on his publication of Ecué-yamba-o in 1933. Some critics regard this work as an ill-advised mixture of socialist realism and Afro-Cuban folklore; the author himself now dismisses it as a flawed attempt at American regionalism, written under a "false conception of what was natural which everyone in my generation shared. "2

Nevertheless, his experiences in Paris served as a literary apprenticeship. He was editor of the famed literary review Imán, which published many contemporary French writers in Spanish translation, and he produced a small book of verse, Poemas de las Antillas, which appeared in Paris in 1932. In 1939 Carpentier returned to Cuba and by 1941 was appointed Professor of History of Music at the National Conservatory. His scholarly investigation of Cuban music led him to publish another work devoted totally to rediscovering from the inside and in colorful detail the essential fabric of his country's culture. 3 He also began writing a series of short stories that would be published in the late 1950s. However, the key event in Carpentier's life was a trip to Haiti in 1943 with the famous French actor Louis Jouvet. It was Haiti that provided Carpentier with the fantastic setting for The Kingdom of This World (1949), his first mature novel and his first international success. Kingdom is a beautifully composed book, revealing a bizarre and brilliant version of Haitian history as a cyclical but never-hopeless process of revolution. In the preface Carpentier admits his new preoccupation with history and his discovery of the "marvellous reality" or lo real maravilloso of Latin America, a land where the frontiers between dream and reality are permanently blurred, because the real is fabulous and the fabulous, real. 4 The Kingdom of This World is a series of tableaux also indicating Carpentier's elaborate style, in which he captures the perpetual movement of events in an ordered but rococo setting. Kingdom established Carpentier's literary promise. In five succeeding novels Carpentier will continue to experiment with narrative structure and develop his personal view of history. The Lost Steps (1953) is a romance characterized by J. B. Priestley as "a work of genius, a

genuine masterpiece, one of the most important works of our
time. " The Hunt (1956) may be called a "political" chronicle;
Explosion in a Cathedral (1962), his best "historical" novel.
Concerto Barroco (1974) is another imaginative historical exercise, and Reasons of State (1974) a brilliant satire.

Carpentier spent much time abroad in Europe and the
Americas. He had been exiled in Venezuela since 1945 and
resided in Caracas in voluntary exile till 1959. At the outbreak of the Castro Revolution, Carpentier returned to his
homeland carrying with him the manuscript of Explosion in a
Cathedral. He has since remained there, founding a coherent
program of action, dutifully participating in the country's cultural activities under the "new" regime and since 1966 has
held the post of Cultural Attaché at the Cuban Consulate in
Paris. Apart from his novels and scholarly music work La
música en Cuba (1946), Carpentier has written a series of
short stories since 1944, collected in War of Time (1958),
and is presently writing a three-volume history of the Cuban
Revolution. Like most of the writers considered in this
book, Carpentier, married to Andrea Esteban, is a nomad;
he currently resides in Paris.

Explosion in a Cathedral is not considered one of the
novels of the "boom" in Latin American literature, but it certainly is a forerunner and best exemplifies Carpentier's cos-
mopolite background and his baroque prose. Explosion is a
burst of creative energy containing some of Carpentier's
best narrative prose. Some critics feel there are promising
passages in the novel, with poetic descriptions intelligently
organized by an "essayist's mind. "[5] Explosion takes place
during the years 1789 and 1808. The French Revolution, as
viewed from several Caribbean islands, is the focal point of
the entire novel, with various interludes taking place in Spain
and France. The characters are all Cubans with the exception of Victor Hugues, a real historical person moving among
the fictional characters created by Carpentier. The novel is
prolific, gargantuan in scope, containing over 350 pages,
with chapters separated by titles from Goya's famous set of
etchings, The Disasters of War. In fact, in the final scene
of the novel, taking place in Madrid on May 2, 1808, two of
the protagonists die in a street fight--Madrilians fighting
against Napoleon's troops, setting off the Spanish Revolution
--and almost appear to be entering one of the most famous
of Goya's paintings. Explosion contains a profusion of sights,
sounds, brilliant atmosphere and a plot filled with adventure,

violence, intrigue, love affairs, and confusion--the confusion
of revolutions, French and Spanish. We witness history in
the making, the illusion of democracy, freedom, the roots of
colonialism implanted in the Caribbean, the disillusions of
false idealizing, the cyclical patterns of history emerging to
envelop the elliptically fictional inventions of Carpentier,
leading his protagonists from their freedom to their eventual
destruction. The breakdown of the century of Enlightenment
with the coming of the French Revolution is related to us
through the adventures of a single family left orphaned by
the death of a Cuban merchant. They are Carlos and Sofía,
brother and sister, and their cousin Esteban.

        Seven long chapters divide a sequence of forty-seven
sections that record revolutionary tumult and worse in a wide
variety of settings in Europe (Paris, Bayonne, Madrid) and
America, culminating in the rising against the French in
Madrid on May 2, 1808. We are introduced to the image of
the guillotine, its "diagonal blade gleaming" being transported
by ship from Europe to the New World, a silent but lethal
protagonist observed by the narrator Esteban (or Carpentier):
an image that sets the scene for the bloodshed to follow. At
the novel's inception a Cuban merchant has just died, leaving
his son and daughter and a nephew to fend for themselves.
The abrupt removal of parental authority is the signal for a
new life for the children; they explore the house, play practical jokes, and fall under the influence of the mysterious
Victor Hugues, who introduces them to "fashionable" ideas
of emancipation and freemasonry. Note how Carpentier captures Carlos's feelings of isolation with almost Proustian
sensitivity:

> At last breathing in an aroma he liked and which
> alternated with the smoke from another coffee
> roasting machine at work near a chapel, Carlos
> thought sadly of the life of routine that now awaited
> him. His music would be silenced and he would be
> condemned to live in this marine city, an island
> within an island where every possible outset to ad-
> venture was stepped up by the sea ... (p. 14).

        In Carlos and Sofía's home hangs a huge painting by
an unknown Neopolitan master who confounded all the laws
of plastic art by representing the apocalyptic immobilization
of a catastrophe. It was called "Explosion in a Cathedral,"
this vision of a great colonnade shattering into fragments in
mid-air, pausing a moment as its lines broke, floating so

as to fall better, before it dashed its tons of stone on to the
terrified people underneath.   It is this recurring image in
the painting that prophesies the revolution that is forever in
Carlos, Sofía and Esteban's consciousness as the novel moves
toward its cataclysmic conclusion.   Sofía is convent-educated;
since her father's death she has become a mother to Esteban
and head of their household and later mistress of Victor
Hugues, who seduces her on a sea voyage they take to Haiti
after Sofía's house and world crumble before her very eyes
in Cuba.   When Victor Hugues first meets the orphaned children they are innocents, naïve to any concerns outside of
their own home.   When Esteban, an asthmatic, falls violent-
ly ill, Dr. Ogé, under Victor's influence, is sought out.
The children must ride from their home into the harbor,
into a world of mulattos and mulatas de tal, a world so
strange to them that they see it as a vision of hell, unlike
anything they ever experienced.   Sofía's sexual and intellectual enlightenment proceed in concert to those of her brother
and cousin under the tutelage of Victor Hugues, who himself
represents the new tide of the Age of Enlightenment, bring-
ing rebellious ideas and revolution with him into their Cuban
homeland.   When revolutionary uprisings take place Sofía and
Carlos remain in Cuba while Esteban follows Victor to
Europe and the revolution.   Hugues, an admirer of Robes-
pierre, is sent to Guadeloupe to take over the island and to
convey there the first guillotine.   Esteban accompanies him
as his secretary, witnesses the degeneration of this idealist--
who defends his ideals by bloodshed but once his ideals fall,
feels nothing but cynicism. [7]   Nevertheless, the revolutionary
ideology had taken hold of all three.

> Freemason!   The word flared up and burst out
> again with a terrifying sound.   Freemason! which
> sounded like an explosion in a cathedral (p. 63).

The novel traces Carlos, Sofía, and Esteban's movements from Cuba to other Caribbean ports and to Europe,
as well as their intellectual enrichment and eventual disillusionment with the "age of science."   When they arrive in
Haiti they find Port-au-Prince in the throes of bloody revolution.   Although they are witnessing the birth of a new humanity, it is essentially Esteban who is Carpentier's porte-
parole, who witnesses the European enlightenment, becomes
a revolutionary, and finally diminishes, loses all his individ-
uality, and is swallowed by the events over which he has
little control.   The major strength of the novel lies in
Esteban's ruminations, his critical propensities, and his

disillusionment, which is narrated fully among all the "events" of this panoramic novel.   But it is not easy to trace a single character's thought patterns because of Carpentier's somewhat baroque style.   This style, however, enriches the flow of the narrative with a profusion of events, characters, and places, allowing Carpentier the full scope of his frequent magnificent prose passages.   One notes Esteban's exploration of the sea life of a region and how he comes upon an ideal world, a world untouched by symmetry and geometry, a world of pure creation:[8]

> Out of the sea at the mercy of lunar cycles--
> fickle, furious or generous, curling and dilating,
> forever ignorant of modules, theorems and equa-
> tions--there appeared these surprising shells,
> symbolizing in number and proportion exactly what
> the Mother lacked, concrete examples of linear
> development, of the laws of convolution, of a
> wonderfully precise conical architecture, of
> masses in equilibrium, of tangible arabesques
> which hinted at all the baroquisms to come.   Con-
> templating a snail--a single snail--Esteban re-
> flected on how, for millenium upon millenium, the
> spiral had been present to the everyday gaze of
> maritime races, who were still incapable of under-
> standing it, or even grasping the reality of its
> presence.   He meditated on the prickly husk of
> the sea-urchin, the helix of the mollusc, the
> fluting of the Jacobean scallop-shell, astonished
> by this science of form which had been exhibited
> for so long to a humanity that still lacked eyes to
> appreciate it.   What is there round about me which
> is already complete, recorded, real, yet which I
> cannot understand?   What sign, what message,
> what warning is there, in the curling leaves of the
> endive, the alphabet of moss, the geometry of the
> rose-apple?   Contemplate a snail--a single snail.
> Te deum (p. 180).

Carpentier's objective is to show humanity's poverty of ideas set in the midsts of the wealth of nature, still rich and unknown.

Carpentier's historical perspective adds much to his recreation of events and atmosphere--for example, his rendition of the siege of Guadeloupe.   He even captures the very odor of the victories in the Caribbean: "Victory, that was good. But better than that, tonight there would be fresh hams, studded with cloves of garlic ..." (p. 133). Carpentier is a vigorous writer, masculine, vibrant. It is incongruous that his chief protagonist, the intellectual Esteban, is not stronger, more virile. However, Victor, Carlos, and Esteban are all literary creations of the author's own cosmos and represent particular facets of character. Esteban, for example, will always be sensitive: "I dreamed of such a different revolution," he murmurs after witnessing the ravage of the guillotine under Victor Hugues's tutelage. Carpentier notes his disenchantment repeatedly: "When he returned to Port-au-Prince, Esteban felt a stranger to the times he lived in: a stranger in a remote and bloody world, where everything seemed absurd" (p. 164). And yet in the midsts of his inner emotional turmoil Carpentier writes some of the most beautiful baroque descriptions ever accorded to the thoughts of a leading character:

> Amidst a growing economy of zoological forms,
> the coral forests preserved the earliest baroque
> of Creation, its first luxuriance and extravagance,
> niding their treasures where, in order to see them,
> the young man had to imitate the fish he had once
> been, before he was shaped by the womb--regretting
> the gills and tail which would have enabled him to
> choose these gorgeous landscapes as his permanent
> dwelling-place. In these coral forests Esteban saw
> a tangible image, a ready--and yet so inaccessible--
> configuration, of a Paradise Lost, where the trees,
> barely named as yet by the torpid, hesitant tongue
> of the Man-child, would be endowed with the ap-
> parent immortality of this sumptuous flora, this
> ostensory, this burning bush, where autumn and
> spring could be detected only in a variation of the
> colours, or a slight shifting of the shadows (p.
> 176).

If one were to characterize Carpentier's writing, it is the ambitious scope of his narrative that sustains his readers in almost all of his novels and especially in Explosion in a Cathedral. Carpentier obviously gives great attention to his choice of words, whatever the subject or thematic matter of his prose. Like an oil painter, Carpentier has created with words an ambitious portrait of the sea:

> The pale-green sea had become the colour of ivy,
> opaque and ever more turbulent, and then changed

from inky-green to smoky-green. The old salts
sniffed the gusts, knowing there would be a different smell about them from the dark shadows bear-
ing quickly down on the ship and the abrupt lulls,
broken by warm showers, whose drops were so
heavy that they seemed to be made of mercury.
Towards dusk the moving column of a waterspout
came in sight, and the ships went from crest to
crest as if held in the palm of a hand, and were
scattered in the darkness, their navigation lights
lost to view. They were running now across the
frenzied ebulliency of a sea stirred up of its own
free-will, which struck them head on and from the
beam, hurling itself broadside against the hull; and
even by rapid straightening of the helm they could
not avoid the onslaughts, which swept the deck
from side to side once they were no longer head-
on to the seas (p. 193).

It is obvious that Carpentier writes from his own experiences
and with an authentic artist's perspective. It is the nuggets
of descriptions of experiences he himself has lived that
charge this historical novel (the story line of which is de-
ceptively simple) with its attractiveness. For when Esteban's great adventure is over and he decides to return to
Cuba the novel collapses into a stream of sequential events.
Sofía, who had married a rich merchant, Jorge, is widowed
and returns to Victor Hugues, who is now in charge of
Cayenne. We witness Sofía's disillusion with Victor as the
narrative moves to its conclusion. The power of the church
is restored; slavery is reinstituted in Cayenne. Esteban returns to Cuba and is reunited with Sofía in their old home.

Esteban suddenly stopped, stirred to the very
depths, in front of the "Explosion in a Cathedral"
by the anonymous Neapolitan master. In it were
prefigured, so to speak, so many of the events he
had experienced that he felt bewildered by the
multiplicity of interpretations to which this pro-
phetic, anti-plastic, un-painterly canvas, brought
to the house by some mysterious chance, lent itself. If, in accordance with the doctrines he had
once been taught, the cathedral was a symbol--
the ark and the tabernacle--for his own being,
then an explosion had certainly occurred there,
which, although tardy and slow, had destroyed
altars, images, and objects of veneration. If the

cathedral was the Age, then a formidable explosion had indeed overthrown its most solid walls, and perhaps buried the very men who had built the infernal machine beneath an avalanche of debris. If the cathedral was the Christian Church, then Esteban noticed that a row of sturdy pillars remained intact, opposite those which were shattering and falling in this apocalyptic painting, as if to prophesy resilience, endurance and a reconstruction, after the days of stars foretelling disasters had passed.

"You always liked looking at that picture, " said Sofía, "I think its absurd and nasty" (p. 253).

One sees Esteban's growth and maturity. Although Sofía would prefer to "go back as we were before, " Esteban realizes it is impossible. Near the novel's conclusion Esteban finally exposes his vulnerability, his passion, his driving sexual need for Sofía--to the latter's dismay. "You've spoilt everything, you've destroyed everything" (p. 270). When Jorge dies of a fever, Sofía wants to return to Cayenne. But Carlos persuades her to accompany him to Europe. Esteban is arrested, as Cuba once more is in the throes of revolution. Sofía escapes to Cayenne only to find an older, fatter Victor Hugues. Their reunion is cause for Carpentier's lyrical exposition:

> The language of the two lovers went back to the roots of language itself, to the bare word, to the stammered single word which lay behind all poetry--a word of thanksgiving for the heat of the sun, for the river overflowing on to the newly-turned soil, for the seed accepted by the furrow, for the corn that stood straight as a bobbin. The word was born from their contact, as elemental and pure as the act which generated it. The rhythm of their bodies was so closely adjusted to the rhythms of Creation that a sudden rainstorm, the flowering of plants in the night or a change in the direction of the wind was enough for their desire to well up at dawn or at twilight, enough for their bodies to feel that they had come together in a new climate, in an embrace which re-created the splendour of their first meeting (p. 313).

However, Sofía's happiness with Victor is short-lived. When

slavery is restored in Cayenne, Sofía, realizing this institution has been the basic error of colonialism, can no longer live in a simulacrum of Europeanized society. The Egyptian disease finally arrives in Cayenne, the fever that killed her merchant husband Jorge, now ready to claim her lover Victor Hugues. But Victor survives the ordeal, and Sofía, tired of slavery, death, and revolution, wants to leave. "So this is the end?" he asked. "There's nothing left for us?" "Yes. We were strong right up to the end," replied Sofía (p. 336).

The novel ends on May 2, 1808, in Madrid. Sofía has sailed to Bordeaux and had been living in Madrid. Esteban, escaped from Cuba, has met up with Sofía. Together they live there "in a quiet and affectionate intimacy." Carlos has come from Cuba in search of his sister. In these last pages of the novel Carlos is interviewing people about the Cubans who live together in the Casa de Arcos, the time the entire population of Madrid, and with them Sofía and Esteban, had poured into the streets to protest Napoleon and the French invasion of Spain. "Neither Sofía nor Esteban ever returned to the Casa de Arcos. No further trace of their resting place was ever found" (p. 349). Carpentier brilliantly closes his novel with this passage:

> When the last door had closed, the picture of the "Explosion in a Cathedral," which had been left behind--perhaps deliberately left behind--ceased to have any subject; the bituminous darkness merged it with the dark crimson brocade covering the main wall of the drawing-room, and the scattered and falling columns became invisible against a background which, even now that the light had gone, retained the colour of blood (p. 349).

What better way to begin a book of criticism on the Latin American narrative than with one of the finest examples of the genre? Carpentier indeed has fused novelistic technique with the vital experience of Latin America. Explosion in a Cathedral is a passionate work, vibrant with exotic images, colorful, full of the grandeur and sweep of a traditional eighteenth-century historical novel but narrated with a contemporary awareness. Explosion is a long, rich, episodic novel about the roots of colonialism in the Caribbean and contains the sights, smells, and sounds of Latin America, shows Cubans in search of their own mythic roots in the Caribbean. It is an intelligent work containing a unique stylistic device--quotations from Goya's etchings, which in

the novel's final scene are utilized to brilliant effect, when
Esteban and Sofía die in the street fight against Napoleon's
troops and almost appear to enter one of Goya's most
famous canvasses. In the opinion of Anderson-Imbert,

> Explosion is a brilliant historical novel with bril-
> liant atmosphere, an intelligent selection of events,
> an original perspective, well-drawn characters, a
> plot filled with adventures, violence, intrigues,
> love affairs. The analysis of the revolutionary
> process is impressive; advances and retreats in
> political action, uneven rhythms in the metropolis
> and the colonies, heros who fall, opportunists who
> climb, cynics who persist obstinately in their posi-
> tions, the maimed, the disillusioned, the
> enthusiasts--in short, a picture which Carpentier
> must have known personally in the revolutions he
> witnessed. [9]

Victor Hugues gives Explosion its strictly historical
dimension, but the novel is mainly a chronicle of family
fortunes artistically conceived by Carpentier in cosmic time.
Just as a variety of his artistic or literary perceptions can
be crammed into a single sentence as evidence of his baroque
style, so can great historical experiences. He reduces the
Spanish Revolution to a total of four lines and the individual
tragedy of Esteban and Sofía to a mere detail in a great and
rather simple pattern. [10] Yet because of the wealth of em-
bellishment, the over-use of pictorial effects that clutter the
scenes, causing a somewhat dense texture, Explosion is a
hard novel to penetrate despite the simple conclusions. The
novel is one that appeals more to the mind than to the emo-
tions, [11] and the reader's involvement is minimal.

As fiction, Explosion is among the last of historical
novels ever to come out of Latin America. Many choose to
read into it a critique of the Cuban Revolution of 1959.
Other critics, like Luis Harss, believe the descendants of
Esteban and Sofía or their nameless doubles are alive in
Cuba today, once more arraigned before the tribunal of history, perhaps waiting to be sacrificed again. [12] Preferring
to sidestep these political innuendos, I choose to view the
"image" of Carpentier's fictional premise as his rendition
of history expressed through his fictional or semifictional
personages and not to believe that the author is an apologist
for any particular political ideology. It is Carpentier's fictional way of dealing with history that gives his narrative a

"magical" quality.[13]   Carpentier's magic for me resides in his talent as a writer.

There is nothing distinctly Cuban about Carpentier's writing; he is a cosmopolitan jack-of-all-trades, at home on both sides of the Atlantic.   Of all his novels, Explosion is truly a poetic work of art, the work of a baroque stylist. "The texture of his descriptions is as rich and heavy as brocade, closely wrought with both fantastic and realistic details and figurations, with scenes filled to the point of bursting their seams by his panoramic approach. ...   The materials are so rich that ... the reader thinks he is witnessing the hard-packed material of a hundred novels."[14]

Perhaps it is Alejo Carpentier's sophistication and compulsively idiosyncratic prose style that have won him a wide circle of admirers, as well as his essentially European view of Latin America.[15]   Or because Carpentier "has interwoven the telluric element in his novels with the elucidation of the epic and the political in a creative undertaking of singular significance within the Spanish-American novel ..., reaching toward the universal"[16] that has won him international acclaim.   Carlos Fuentes, in his critical work The New Spanish-American Novel, best sums up Carpentier's worth as a writer: The novels of Carpentier "belong to universal narrative accomplishment, to movements of renovation, which substitute for the conventions of characters and plot as crucial a fusion in which character and intrigue cease to be central and become buffers for a language that is ... real."[17]   While reading Carpentier, one feels part of an "authentic world where there still exist positive values such as the deep collective consciousness of myths and the past, the certainty of man's identity and a life style attuned to natural rhythms...."[18]   "Carpentier mixes legend and fact, mythology and history and experiments with temporal magic, music, allegory and surrealism to create an ironic picture, tempered by brutality and blood."[19]

Explosion in a Cathedral utilizes all sorts of stylistic effects--interior monologue, first- and third-person narration.   However, Carpentier's "style is submerged in his end product--a completely believable, warm, sensual and magic world."[20]   Other critics felt Explosion was a "curiously evasive achievement ..., dramatizing the contradicting allegiances between private sensibility and public ideology. Though its setting was the Antilles of the eighteenth century, most readers took the setting for what it is--pure Zanuck

cum Goldwyn. "[21]   Above all, Explosion is an entertainment,
written with sensibility in the best pictorial tradition of the
Hollywood screenplay, such as Walter Wanger's The Black
Book (1949), Darryl F. Zanuck's Son of Fury (1942), and
Samuel Goldwyn's The Hurricane (1937), although it is much
closer philosophically and politically to Gilo Pontecorvo's
Burn! (1963).

Carpentier's novel deserves to be read, with its
author's flair for developing character and description in a
historical setting as well as his fertile imagination.   But
baroque stylists sometimes exceed their limitations.   Carpentier's latest translated novel, Reasons of State (1976),
did not fare very well with American critics precisely because of its tedium, its pages and pages of lists of objects
and sensations that do not advance the cause of narrative or
character, and its poor mixture of politics and comedy. [22]

Although Carpentier's later novels do contain much
tiresome philosophy, Explosion represents the almost perfect
marriage of history and fiction.   It has drive, a sweeping
panorama, depth, perception, and artistry; its enduring
symbolic title has cinematic references--for the "explosion"
is the Spanish Revolution caught in a "freeze" frame.   Carpentier suggests a static portrait.   It will take the "unfreez-
ing" or a greater war effort to liberate the Western hemis-
phere from its French oppressors.   For Latin America is a
marvellous setting, a literary miracle on which Carpentier
has built his career.   The concept of the "marvellous" is
part of the mythical image of America, and Carpentier
proselytizes for belief in the reality of the marvellous, a
cultural reality in spite of a real or "objective" reality.
Carpentier's idea--that the reality of the marvellous is the
guiding romanticized mythical image of America--gives
Explosion its strength, its primitive character, its notion of
triumph, its goodness.   For Carpentier writes with a French
sensibility and a dense baroque style tempered by innocence.
He is a modern-day Chauteaubriand, a master stylist, a giant
among contemporary Latin American novelists.

2. CORTAZAR: ARGENTINE INTELLECTUAL CONJURER

Born in Brussels, Belgium, on August 26, 1914, of Argentine parents, Julio Cortázar's literary reputation is based mainly on his short stories and on his highly experimental novels Hopscotch (1963) and A Manual for Manuel (1973). Although several of his short stories have inspired screenplays and films by such noted directors as Michelangelo Antonioni (Blow-up) and Jean-Luc Godard (Week-end), his novels have not as yet reached the cinematic marketplace. Cortázar lived in Belgium until he was four years old and then moved back to Argentina, where he resided with his middle-class parents, Julio and María (Descotte) Cortázar, in Banfield, a suburb of Buenos Aires. His father, however, deserted the family, and the youngster was brought up in a home dominated by women. His mother reared and educated him at some sacrifice. From 1926 to 1936 he attended Buenos Aires Teachers College and in 1932 earned a degree as an elementary-school teacher. In 1935 he earned another degree as a secondary-school teacher, and in 1936 he passed his first-year examinations at the University.

Although a desire to study in Europe was frustrated by his family, at age eighteen Cortázar remained at the University and became a teacher of French literature, working mainly in the provinces of Bolivar and Chiuilco and later in Buenos Aires. This abortive attempt to study in Europe became the inspiration for his first novel, The Winners (1960). However, before becoming a novelist, Cortázar had begun his literary apprenticeship as an essayist, poet, translator, and short-story writer.

To recount here the large number of his early publications would be fruitless, although several generalizations

14

about the formation of his intellect are worth making.
Cortázar spent many of his youthful years reading a great
amount of contemporary French and English literature, following the interests of his contemporary Jorge Luis Borges,
with whose critical interests he identified early in his
career. Cortázar began his true literary career in the
Literature Department of the University of Buenos Aires.
Throughout the 1940s he published forgettable volumes of
poetry, taught French-literature courses, and became a
public translator--a career that served him well, since today he resides in Paris, holds French citizenship, and
works primarily as a translator for UNESCO.

   During the 1940s Cortázar was jailed for protesting
the Perón regime, and in 1951 he left Argentina for good.
Since he could no longer teach under a dictatorship,
Cortázar became an intellectual émigré and, although a
French citizen, a defender of Fidel Castro's Cuban revolution and the Allende regime in Chile, thus atoning, perhaps,
for his own lack of political commitment in the 1940s and
50s. Leftist and neo-Peronista groups in Argentina have
severely criticized him because of his French citizenship
and because he appears to be divorced from his native
country. Yet Argentina is usually the theme of his short-
story collections and his novels. According to David
Foster, "Cortázar's works evoke the texture of Argentine
life, particularly the ironies, stupidities and dangerous
limitations of a middle-class that was once considered the
hope and promise of Latin America."[1]

   His career as a short-story writer began in earnest
with the publication of Bestiary in 1951. Subsequently he
has published Cronopios and Famas (1953), End of the Game
and Other Stories (1956), Secret Weapons (1958), All Fires
the Fire (1966), and Octadero (1974). Consistent with his
steady production of short stories has been his pursuit of
the novel genre. The Winners (1960) was his first full-
length novel, a parable of modern life in the form of a
ship's voyage begun as the result of a lottery. It was
Hopscotch (1963), characterized as an "anti-novel" with
interchangeable parts, that was his international literary
breakthrough, just when the "boom" was gathering momentum.

   Hopscotch is an extremely complex novel, "explicitly
repudiating the conventional form of the narrator, symboliz-
ing in its erratic order of reading the illogical progress of

men through life and the irrational search of meaning and truth through the traditional chronological sequence. "2   The entire novel is an elaborate game, a puzzle in which the reader participates.   Its theme is anarchy in a world where order is absurd.   The reader may read the novel in a traditional manner, in a sequential order of pages, or may hopscotch, at the author's suggestion, flipping from chapter to chapter, following the author's sequence.   Hopscotch is a brilliant, complex, and labyrinthian novel.

Cortázar followed the success of Hopscotch with two other highly experimental novels: 62, A Model Kit (1968) and A Manual for Manuel (1973).   Like Hopscotch, A Manual for Manuel is also set in Paris and is a study of events that goes beyond the surface appearance of daily phenomena to lay bare the surprising elements that characterize everyday events.   Manual is a collage based on a babybook collection of revolutionary clippings prepared for a child, Manuel, by his mother Susana.   Perhaps A Manual for Manuel was an outgrowth of Cortázar's collage books, Around the Day in Eighty Worlds (1967) and Last Round (1968).

Of particular note is Cortázar's return trip to Argentina to coincide with the publication of A Manual for Manuel.   Cortázar had not been in Latin America in over twenty years; while there he also visited Peru, Ecuador, and Chile.   In 1974 he came to the United States and participated in the Poets, Essayists and Novelists Translation Conference (P. E. N.) and returned a year later to be honored at the University of Oklahoma's Fifth Conference on Writers of the Hispanic World.   A tall, slim, reticent man, somewhat boyish in appearance, Cortázar lives and works in Paris with his wife, the former Aurora Bermúdez.   Both are translators for UNESCO.   Cortázar is a jazz aficionado and also plays the trumpet.   He is currently finishing up a series of over one hundred short pieces, about incidents, places, and people, and he is waiting for translations of his two most recent books of short stories to appear in English.

Although many readers consider Hopscotch the finest novel to come out of Latin America in the 1960s, ranking it above García Márquez's One Hundred Years of Solitude--it is still rife with shortcomings.   In the opinion of Emir Rodríguez Monegal:

Although provocative and brilliant in many respects,

there is scarcely anything in its elaborate theorizing
that is original; the plot lacks interest, the characters do not develop, and the best episodes are
really separate short stories embedded in his
text. [3]

Hopscotch may have introduced a new dimension into Latin
American literature and attracted the reading public of the
early 1960s, but A Manual for Manuel is also experimental
in character and, while suffering from similar limitations,
is a far more clever work, making interesting use of contemporary documentary material.   It has, however, escaped
much of the scrutiny accorded Hopscotch by contemporary
literary critics.

First published in the United States in 1978, A Manual
for Manuel is very much like Hopscotch, with a Parisian
setting and Argentine characters, but is a shorter, more co-
hesive work, and in it Cortázar is interested less in the
inner lives of his characters than in the effect of public
events upon them.   Cortázar has become politicized.   Also
like Hopscotch, Manual is a difficult work, uneasy in its
writing, but surprisingly accessible considering its ambi-
tions and its shorter length, some 389 pages.   Unaccount-
ably, few readers and critics have given attention to Manual,
which is mystifying simply because it may be considered a
sequel of sorts to the famous but difficult Hopscotch.   In
fact, one critic felt that "it is as if Cortázar was determined
that the two novels shouldn't fail to be compared, so that the
differences between them could be better gauged. "[4]

On the dust jacket of its English translation A Manual
for Manuel was hailed as a "liberating book [that] presents a
heroic notion of revolution difficult to realize ... there will
be room in it for Andy Warhol, aleatory music, Rimbaud,
Joni Mitchell and magic. "   Manual's pages are without chapter headings and are interspersed with reproduction of some
fifty newspaper articles (translated from the French by
Cortázar), organizational charts, poetry, interlinear textual
notes, Telex communiqués, and signs--in short, a collage of
messages from various media forming (again, from the dust
jacket)

Cortázar's first political novel as the author applies his special mindscape to today's headlines,
tackling the surreal world of Latin American exiles
in Paris who are intent on committing revolutionary

acts. Using smuggled counterfeit money, they
finance a plan to kidnap a top Latin American
police official, whose headquarters are in Paris,
and hold him for ransom until certain political
prisoners in Latin America are released. [5]

It is Cortázar's first prorevolutionary novel, his
much-awaited literary engagement. The world of Cortázar's
sometimes improbable intellectuals-on-the-run blossoms
amidst pages interspersed with newspaper clippings of jail-
breaks, police attacks, tortures, and assaults on rebellious
youth. The chief characters, Andrés and his girlfriend
Ludmilla, are on the fringe of the revolutionary group,
searching their souls whether to commit themselves or not
to the oncoming revolution. "All his characters are searching for an almost mystical 'bridge' to a revolutionary new
world; but the bridge proves elusive, the revolution far away.
Only Manuel, a baby for whom this manual of clippings and
thoughts is being compiled may live to see its arrival. "[6]

Running concurrently throughout the novel with a kidnapping plot is Andrés's attempt to interpret a dream: while
watching a Fritz Lang film, he is called to the theater's office. A mysterious Cuban commands him to perform an act
that, upon hearing, he cannot remember. This lapse of
memory becomes the "black stain or spot" of the novel.
Andrés vainly tries to interpret his dream, the Fritz Lang
movie (which was probably M or Fury), and feels as if he
were acting within and without the Lang film. The dream
sequence occurs early, within the first hundred pages of the
novel, but significance is revealed thirty pages before the
conclusion.

... it's clear, now that there isn't any black
stain. ... I see my dream as I'm really dreaming
it, so idiotic, so clear, so obvious ... that the
dream was nothing more than that, that the Cuban
was looking at me and saying only two words to
me: Wake up! (p. 359).

Some critics have taken these words to be significant as
Andrés's (Cortázar's) call to awaken to the revolution through
a Freudian catharsis. [7] Andrés finally joins the Joda
(Cortázar's ironic code name for the kidnapping plot, translated as the Screwery); and at the moment of engagement,
after coming to understand the "black spot" of his dream,
he tries to join Marco at the group's hideout and prevents

Ludmilla, his mistress, from helping Marco as the French police storm the hideout.

Manual's conclusion is open-ended and somewhat unclear. What is clear, however, is that the reader must put together the clippings interspersed throughout the novel for the child Manuel. We have been reading the scrapbook (novel) throughout and Cortázar demands our active participation, creating a new novel, a manual (collage) of sorts. Cortázar suggests the failure of this particular revolutionary kidnapping plot but suggests future success of other acts and the revolution itself. John Incledon has noted that "to read Cortázar with any understanding, he requires his readers to perform a structural analysis on his texts...."[8] Cortázar wrote A Manual for Manuel when Structuralism was at its height. Manual, according to Incledon, is "one of the most complex, interesting and successful attempts to bring the Structuralism of Claude Lévi-Strauss into the literary arena."[9]

Written in the tradition of the anti-novel, A Manual for Manuel is Cortázar's best novel to date. Like its predecessor, Hopscotch, it retains all the elements that make a Cortázar novel a vital experience: the magic of dreams and their interpretation, sensuality, sexuality, linguistic forays, humor, biographical elements. One critic even suggested that Manual was written as a parallel to the Parisian section of Hopscotch.

> The Club of expatriates in the French capital with
> their distinctive cultural enthusiasms (Fritz Lang,
> Hindu philosophy, and so on), reappears as the
> less decorous group named "La Joda." As the
> male pair between whom the author locates himself,
> Oliveira and Traveler are replaced by Marcos and
> Andrés; the female duo La Maga-Talita, by Lud-
> milla-Francine. We even have a replay of the
> boy-child undertone, Rocamadour surviving longer
> now as the (Im)manuel for whom the book within
> the book is created.[10]

The key to understanding this novel is how the main characters (Andrés, Ludmilla, Francine, Lonstein, Marcos, Patricio, and Susana) deal with the information they are clipping for Manuel's scrapbook. The clippings are a compendium of political and sexual acts, having repercussions for the fictional characters and indicating the political agonies

of present-day Latin America. Most stirring is the eleven-
page excerpt from Mark Lane's Conversations with Americans, specifically dealing with the methods and brutality in-
flicted by Americans during the Vietnam war with expressed
government sanction. In a note specifically for American
readers of this novel Cortázar refers to "oppression and repression that appear in the course of the novel in Argentina
and other Latin American countries [which is] still in effect
during composition of this book" (p. 5).

A Manual for Manuel also reads like a hippie-yippie
manifesto. There are vulgar word games intertwined everywhere in the text, references to "mushrooms," hallucinogens,
sexual liberation, use of drugs, maté, orgies, heterosexual-
ity, homosexuality, bisexuality, ménages à trois, masturba-
tion, onanism, and linguistic treatises on the words penis,
vagina, buttocks, and many more. A utopian, Cortázar feels
we must drop all our present societal taboos and make
friends with everyone and everything. Yet there is a certain
glossiness about Cortázar's novel, a kind of depersonalization
and special irony in that the author himself is a French citizen and no longer a Latin American expatriate. One reviewer felt that "the narrator himself is more worried about the
best way to write his book than about toppling a distant dictatorship. [The book certainly] makes generous and amusing
fiction, but poor futurology."[11] The disjointed narrative is
full of absurdities, with many things going on at the same
time. John Leonard:

> a turquoise penguin flown to Paris by jet from
> Argentina; the stealing of nine thousand wigs,
> steamy sex scenes, "black humor" eroticism, a
> sort of cerebral thrashing to get at the senses. . . .
> It will be a revolution that renders the world safe
> for homosexuals and gratuitous acts, a polymor-
> phous perverse revolution. It will liberate Manuel.
> It asks too much, of us and of itself.[12]

The novel's greatest problem is the validity of
its premise, that a group of Latin American expatriate intellectuals plan a kidnapping in Paris cafés and dingy hotel
rooms, drinking maté and listening constantly to Stock-
hausen's "Prozession." Manual's plot is certainly colorful
but not totally believable; one critic felt the novel had its
genesis in "something as vulgar as guilt,"[13] since Cortázar
has been severely criticized by his Latin American compa-
triots for his indifference to his fellow Argentines. But

Cortázar maintains that it is important to separate political opinions from fiction.   In an interview with Frank MacShane, he states:

> But whereas in Hopscotch I was mainly interested in the inner lives and relationships of characters, in this new book [Manual], I am concerned with the effect of public events on them ... so I had to try to establish an equilibrium between the private lives and public events ... with some humor and to use comedy.[14]

Another problem in Manual is that the characters never really react to the articles they are reading or translating: they merely place them in a scrapbook.   Another difficulty is one of thematic focus.   Is Manual a political work or a sexual one?   Cortázar states that Manual has a lot to do with sex in Latin America.   "I try to go into that subject as far as I can and to deal with machismo and with notions of male superiority.   This on top of other things is what the book is about."[15]

Whatever the subject of Manual, it is certainly an experience, "a rich experience which opens up many issues and lets them unfold."[16]   With this novel (as well as his others), Cortázar feels that he is writing about authentic material in the realm of his own heritage.   He and his fellow "boom" writers will no longer be accused of being imitators, but have "turned inward to discover the roots of their own being" and thus have "ended literary colonialism in South America."[17]

Winner of the Prix Medicis, Manual represents one of the best examples of a novel written in the "boom" tradition.   But it goes even further.   It establishes Cortázar as a political person trying to carry out his own belief in the future world of socialism without belonging to any political party.   Reading Manual is like solving a puzzle--Cortázar's world is labyrinthian--but unlike Hopscotch, Manual has an easily identifiable center.   Manual proffers an incandescent tension, a vision of liberty unattained, a wry way of implying much with little.

Cortázar is an excellent writer with an excellent ear. His own translation expertise operates throughout the novel, capturing the modulations of dialect and intonation.   Manual strains for meanings within the chaos of its narrative, in a renovated style that is anti-literary, a literature of multiple perspectives, fragmented, kaleidoscopic, open-ended. Cortázar is like an orchestrator, smashing the score (narrative) and reordering the fragments in such a way as to render apparent the underlying order, his own "silent performance."[18] Cortázar forces us to create our own myths, and we become an audience of silent performers, activated by the author's carefully chosen allusions, creating our own reality "to change reality for everyone ... to meld the real with mankind.... Consequence: there's only one duty and that's to find the true course. Method: revolution. Yes" (p. 9). And with revolution comes death, despair (but with promises of regeneration), and the failure of love. Manual is a novel of hope and despair, struggle and liberation. For Andrés's struggle is part of Cortázar's relentless effort to liberate humanity and create a new kind of humanism. All his works are ultimately "a route seeking to arrive at a center, at a final island, at a world that exists in this one but that one has to create like the phoenix."[19] There are no easy final answers for Cortázar, "a non-conformist, a rebel, a poet who searches through literature to earn the right to enter the house of man."[20]

One worthwhile note from Gregory Rabassa, Cortázar's talented translator, demands inclusion here:

> ... in A Manual for Manuel we can see that words are the real liars, that the truth is found in what is left unsaid.... Cortázar's fictions then must be taken in the same spirit they are written and that the unwritten has as much significance as what has been articulated, perhaps even more.[21]

Each reading of Manual also suggests a greater opening up, a greater participation of a character and the reader, a duality of language for participation, both reader and author sharing a text, leading to action and reaction. Saul Sosnowski views Cortázar's best two novels from this point of view:

> In the cases of both Hopscotch and A Manual for Manuel it is not so much the collages of Western ideas, of daily acts of terrorism, which linger after having read them, but the overlapping of these notions into a language which denounces them and which allows, or awaits, their destruction.[22]

Cortázar's anti-novels make a great impact on their readers, the author's "language of denunciation" hopefully precipating a combative response.

One critic felt Cortázar wrote his Manual in order to expose the systematic torture of political prisoners in many Latin American countries. [23]   (It is interesting to note in this context that the author has used his royalties to help the families of political prisoners.)   Yet Manual is not a political novel.   It is an entertainment, "a bizarre mixture of fantasy and fact ... told from a confused perspective of Andrés and another member of the group known as 'you know who,'"[24] probably Cortázar himself.   The plot of Manual is so hysterically imaginative, the characters of "La Joda" so wild, their pranks so humorous, their eroticism so prevalent, that at times it seems to overwhelm the political focus of the novel, leading one to the feeling that Cortázar wrote Manual first as an entertainment, albeit one with political overtones.   Yet Manual's documentary sections can also be taken as a bit of shock therapy to underscore the United States' role in aiding oppressive regimes by training police in torture tactics.   In an interview with Evelyn Picon Garfield, Cortázar "maintained he was also strongly indicting Latin Americans for brutalizing against their own brothers."[25]

Apart from drawing us into the political arena, Cortázar's novels are entertaining, leavened with great wit, displaying a unique imagination, an urbane, sophisticated intellectual's grasp of a variety of subjects but mostly on sexuality and politics.   Cortázar conjures an entire world with the playfulness of a necromancer.   "A Manual for Manuel is a remarkable book ... it is a running plea for saving frivolity in the midst of serious concerns."[26]   Cortázar's characters never sacrifice their personal freedom, erotic rites, aesthetic preferences, imagination, or humor for an ideology.   It is to their playfulness that American readers will most respond and ultimately admire in Cortázar's flawed masterpiece.

3.   LEZAMA LIMA: CUBAN SEXUAL PROPENSITIES

It is appropriate that Julio Cortázar has provided us with an
introduction to Lezama Lima's work in a eulogy written in
1976.   Like Cortázar, Lezama was a spiritual exile, a sensitive poet-novelist, geographically tied to Cuba for almost
all of his sixty-six years.

> Apparently inclined toward the most remote part of
> a universal past--between the real and the mythic--
> Lezama diligently sought out the roots of the Cuban
> present, of the Cuban individual.   By doing so, he
> shed light on the mental subsoil, the deep strata of
> Latin America, and that illumination is future, not
> past; mission, not gratuitous game; revolutionary
> work, not elitist literature....   If I found myself
> forced to reread just one Latin American novel,
> that novel would be Paradiso.   ... it consoles me
> to know that that book is a book born in the earth
> and out of Cuban soil--a powerful beacon of beauty
> and of presentiment and of arrival. [1]

José María Andrés Fernando Lezama Lima was born
in the garrison of Columbia in Havana, Cuba, on December
19, 1910.   He lived there all of his life except for two short
trips to Mexico and Jamaica in 1949 and 1950.   He almost
never left Cuba because of his asthma; he lived with his
mother, surrounded by a very small group of devoted disci-
ples.   "He was a pampered and sickly child, suffering from
asthma at an early age," says Monegal.   "Lezama Lima
grew up in a traditional Cuban family, spoiled by his mother
and grandmother and in loving conflict with a stern father, a
Captain in Cuba's army. "[2]

He was chiefly known as a poet who wrote in a

24

hermetic and, later, a surrealist style. His first books of
poems were published in the late 1930s and early 1940s:
The Death of Narcissus (1937), Inimical Murmuring (1941),
and Secret Adventures (1945); he continued to publish poetry
throughout his life: Fixity (1949), Arístides Fernández (1950),
Giver (1962), Imaginary Eras (1971), and his Complete
Poetry (1972). He was a master poet; according to Anderson-
Imbert, "the ascendancy which he exercises over other writers seems due to the example of a life monstrously conse-
crated to literature. Moreover, a life made up of books,
bibliophilistic and bookish."[3] He cofounded and contributed
to a variety of literary magazines in Cuba, among them
Verbum (1937), Espuela de plata (1938-41), Nadie parecía
(1942-44), and Orígines. The latter, which he edited from
1944 to 1957 in collaboration with José Rodríguez Feo,
helped shape the development of Cuban poetry before and
after the 1959 Castro revolution.

Lezama Lima was also a master essayist, and his
total devotion to literature is seen in his bibliomaniac essays Analect of the Watch (1953), The American Expression
(1957), and Tracts in Havana (1958). But it was not until
1966, when Lezama Lima published his first novel, Paradiso,
that he attained intellectual prominence. The book projected
him immediately to fame; up to that time he was known
chiefly to a handful of readers of poetry in Latin America.
Apparently, Lezama's decision to publish Paradiso was influenced by his mother's death in 1964 and his marriage in
1965. In fact, just one year before Paradiso's appearance
Lezama compiled the definitive three-volume Anthology of
Cuban Poetry, affirming his poet's role. He had also published Orbit (1966), which contained, in addition to poetry,
two short stories and some essays, and Los grandes todos
(1968), which included a chapter from the unpublished novel
Fronesis. This chapter probably was integrated in Paradiso
in some form among other excerpts of the novel that appeared in various issues of Orígines. Paradiso itself is an
ambitious, predominantly successful evocation of a poet's
growth through his sensual and spiritual experiences, reaffirming Lezama's dedication to a poet's life.

Before his death in 1976 José Lezama Lima was one
of the directors of Cuba's Union of Artists and Writers and
was honored by the Castro regime with several important
cultural posts, such as Director of the Department of Literature and Publication of the National Cultural Council; but
he is now out of favor, because Paradiso is a novel that

pointedly ignores politics.   The book is a critique of a certain type of bourgeois mentality that the Revolution tried vainly to eradicate; it never even mentions the Revolution, and contains, as well, a frank discussion of homosexuality, a taboo topic in Cuba.

After 1966 several anthologies of poetry and autobiographical treatises and essays by Lezama Lima appeared in Cuba: Anthology (1968), Esfera imagen (1969), A Possible Image of Lezama Lima (1969), A Charmed Life (1970), Introduction to Opening Vessels (1971), and Questioning Lezama Lima (1972).

On a visit to Cuba Julio Cortázar reported that before Lezama's death he had seen the second completed part (the sequel) of Paradiso, entitled Oppiano Licario, as well as a bulky manuscript of poems.   Neither these poems or Oppiano Licario have appeared posthumously, and so the world must await the culmination of "one of the most extreme endeavors of human creation--begun some forty years ago and conducted simultaneously in the fields of poetry, narrative and meditation."[4]   In a recent Literary Letter from Cuba Peter Winn states that Oppiano Licario was published in Cuba in 1977, one year after Lezama's death, although it has not appeared in the United States in Spanish or English at this writing. [5]

As mentioned above, Paradiso is not very popular in Cuba because Lezama Lima's "apolitical pedantry, Baroque poetics and homosexual politics seem out of step with the Cuban revolution."[6]   And yet, "although Paradiso is neither a revolutionary novel, nor a novel of the revolution, it is probably the most important work of fiction written in Cuba since the revolution."[7]   Lezama Lima has been often called the "Cuban Proust, " the poet of Cuban sensuality and the conjurer of Cuban experience.   Winn believes that "he may not have been a government favorite, but the power of his poetry won him respect and admiration that assured the publication of his works."[8]   D. W. Foster reports:

> He is such an important figure that when the students of the University of Havana complained to Castro about the withdrawal of Paradiso from sale because of the demands of a few partisan factions, Fidel ordered that it be put back on sale the following morning.   Lezama Lima has benefited from the revolution to the extent that he has become a national figure without having been forced to change

his work in favor of a great degree of [socialist]
realism. [9]

Paradiso is Lezama Lima's acknowledged masterpiece.
Considered to be one of the few Cuban writers to write about
Cuban themes in a Cuban way, Lezama has also inspired
younger writers who share his quest for Cuban identity and
an authentically Cuban literature. Paradiso was hailed as a
masterpiece by fellow contemporary writers, such as Julio
Cortázar and Mario Vargas Llosa. Besides being "as perceptive and psychologically intricate as Proust, as vigorous
and sometimes corroded as Faulkner's portrait of the
South,"[10] as stylistically intricate as Joyce's Ulysses,
Paradiso is a cosmos, somewhat autobiographical, evoking
the vanished world of the Cuban bourgeoisie, a verbal tap-
estry extraordinarily erotic in character set in a "lush
imagistic style that is simultaneously elegiac and ironic,
erotic and erudite. "[11] In José Cemí, his protagonist, Lezama
has poetically established his fictional counterpart. For,
like Marcel Proust or James Joyce, Lezama has tried to recapture the historical as well as his own personal past; he
is, in the words of Edmund White, "intent upon defeating
time and submerging it into the eternity of art through a
thorough transformation of autobiographical detail and an
artist's penetrating scrutiny";[12] and it is this that has elevated Paradiso to a work of art comparable to Ulysses or
Remembrance of Things Past.

It is indeed difficult to summarize the plot of this
466-page, fourteen-chapter novel; it is a work hardly con-
ducive to meticulous critical analysis, even less to a casual,
straightforward reading. Paradiso is an ambitious evocation
of a poet's development; it contains much interwoven material about Cuban family life that has little to do with the main
thrust of the plot. "Depending upon your taste or tolerance
for elaborate diction, " says White, "you will find Lezama's
style either intoxicating or repellent. "[13] One critic felt
that "in Paradiso, Lezama seems to have two main pur-
poses: to dumbfound us with his erudition and to extend
Góngora's euphemisms into a baroque novel. He succeeds
in both but the novel is impossible. "[14] Even Lezama's
staunch supporter Julio Cortázar felt that to read him was
one of the most arduous and irritating tasks that can be
undertaken and that one should approach the book "by
swimming. "[15]

Paradiso narrates the childhood and adolescence of

its asthmatic hero José Cemí and tells the panoramic history
of the two branches of his family, the Cemís and the Olayas,
as reflected in the genealogical chart placed after the title
page. Its fourteen chapters are divided into two parts, the
first dealing with José Cemí's family and his childhood
through adolescence and the last, his adult life and university years. There are numerous autobiographical elements
in Paradiso, as Klaus Müller-Bergh has observed:

> The novelist, like his hero, is from Havana, suf-
> fers from chronic asthma, descends from a father
> who was head of the military academy of El Morro
> and a mother whose parents were revolutionary
> exiles. Both lost their fathers at an early age in
> an influenza epidemic that swept Cuban and Ameri-
> can forces on military maneuvers in Florida.
> Lezama's mother ... much in the fashion of
> Rialta (Cemí's mother), was expecting a child dur-
> ing the final illness of her husband. After his
> death, the author's family, like that of Cemí,
> moved to the house of the maternal grandmother
> in the Calle Prado of Havana. [16]

The novel is set in and around Havana, from the end
of the nineteenth century through the late 1930s. When we
meet José Cemí in the opening chapter, he is five years old
and suffering from an acute asthmatic attack. Baldovina,
his maid, and her own children appear throughout the novel,
as the Cemí family moves from Cuba to Florida and back
again. In Chapter One we also meet José's father, an army
colonel, his wife Rialta, and her mother Doña Augusta. As
Chapter Two opens it is 1917, and young José is now ten
years old; Chapter Three takes us back to Jacksonville in
1894. The fourth and fifth chapters take us even further
back in time to the early 1880s, recounting José Cemí
Senior's childhood, school days, and adolescence. We see
the colonel woo and win Rialta, and the story of each family's brothers and sisters, with ensuing entanglements, is
also narrated. In Chapter Six we are present at Rialta's
wedding, the birth of our protagonist, and the death of the
colonel at age thirty-three and are introduced to Oppiano
Licario (the subject of Lezama's sequel to Paradiso).
Chapter Seven outlines the effects of the colonel's death on
the Cemí family, specifically José and his sisters Violante
and Eloisa, and introduces Rialta's brothers and sisters with
their problems. We witness Doña Augusta's preparation of
gourmet meals, her illness.

The famous or infamous eighth chapter, dealing essentially with José's adolescence, marks the second half of
Paradiso.   It introduces us to his classmates, especially
Farraluque, a precocious youth known for his indiscriminate
sexual prowess.   We witness the latter's homosexual encounter with Adolfcito, his heterosexual one with a mulata,
his hilarious mastubatory techniques in a coal bin.   Chapter
Eight also introduces Ricardo Fronesis, the son of a law-
yer, who becomes one of José's closest friends with whom
he debates the homosexual question.   Chapters Nine and Ten
are set at the university; Cemí and his friends are in their
twenties; it is a time for student rebellion. Eugenio Foción
at age twenty-five becomes the third part of José's intellectual triumvirate: ". . . he was older than both of them,
about twenty-five, quite thin with hair that was golden and
aggressive, like a falcon" (p. 226).   The three of them discourse on a variety of subjects: the origin of Cervantes'
Quixote, homosexuality, Fronesis's affair with Lucia,
Foción's desire for Fronesis, Nietzsche, and Rialta's
fibroid tumor operation; finally there is an interpolated
short story dealing with Foción's parents, fascinating in itself because it demonstrates the beginning of the latter's
homosexual preferences.   Chapter Eleven reaffirms and
strengthens the bonds of friendship between José Cemí and
Ricardo Fronesis; in fact, in an interpolated poem entitled
"Portrait of José Cemí," we experience José's joy and intellectual rapprochement to Ricardo.   Foción informs the
group of his trip to New York.   We witness Ricardo's
father's attempt to stop any further friendship between his
son and Foción, because of the latter's homosexuality.
Foción is later taken away by Cuban authorities for urinat-
ing in a public place and exposing his genitals.   Fronesis
disappears from the narrative, and José is left alone in
law school.   We witness Doña Augusta's death from cancer
in her eighties.

Chapter Twelve is perhaps the most misunderstood
chapter in the novel since it seems to be an interpolation
of four distinct short stories on the nature of death and
time.   However, Chapters Thirteen and Fourteen pick up
the thread of the narrative and return us to Cuba, to an
episode aboard a bus, where thieves steal some valuable
coins from Oppiano Licario, which are retrieved by José
Cemí.   We witness several surrealist scenes.   For example,
the passengers on the bus also reside in the building where
Licario lives; they play a strange game: "Martincillo, inside a circle, jabbed with his piccolo at a furious crab
which barked like a dog" (p. 422).

The very last chapter reintroduces Oppiano Licario as a link to José Cemí's past (he saw his father die) and resolves in a somewhat open-ended fashion young José's problems with Fronesis and Foción. The novel closes with a poem written by Licario entitled "José Cemí," ending "I saw your father die; and now Cemí, stumble." The very last line of the novel suggests another whole volume the subject of which will be Licario's legacy and psychological relationship with José--"... now we can begin" (p. 466).

I have purposely left out a multiplicity of characters and subplots, sexual encounters, philosophic treatises on time, literature, religion, gourmet cooking, Cuban foods, etc., and briefly tried to describe the main events in José Cemí's world. There are also many lengthy descriptions of the Cemí home, the colonel's study, his books, desk, engineering papers, a total world among the many described by Lezama. "Lezama Lima creates an entire world," writes Raymond Souza, "and he does so, in part, by his attempts to portray the total essences of his characters and their surroundings."[17] The principal theme of the novel is essentially José's "search for a basic understanding of the world and the universe, ... from unawareness to awareness, from multiplicity to unity, from chaos to form and order."[18]

There have been many interpretations of Paradiso. Souza, in his excellent book Modern Cuban Novelists, devotes an entire chapter to Paradiso. He makes these essential points:

> Paradiso can be considered as a set of spirals converging in a circle. ... rather than being a symbol of unity, the circle is used as a means of conveying the search for meaning that each individual must experience in his life, with its attendant confusion and chaos.... The geometric progression from a square to a circle also appears during the sexual encounters ... the search for meaning in life and control over chaos.[19]

Foción's bisexual activities are a symbol of chaos; Fronesis is always in control of his life, while José moves toward fuller control and comprehension of his direction in the future through his experiences with his friends. Besides the circular motion of the novel, other prime themes are death, time, and creativity. Many critics have discussed

the significance of Paradiso's last three chapters, especially
Chapter Twelve with its interpolation of four separate short
stories: the first is a Roman episode dealing with a soldier's struggle against death; the second explores the relationship of a grandmother and small child; the third deals
with an anonymous narrator wandering through Havana, delv-
ing into the mysteries of existence; the fourth concerns Juan
Longo, an aging musician whose young wife is trying to defeat
the ravages of time by placing him in a cataleptic trance.
All four stories concern the human struggle against time.
Although somewhat peripheral to José Cemí's own plight,
they represent Lezama's creative approach and, according
to Souza, a "unified view of reality.   As a result, the reader experiences a movement from multiplicity to unity as the
fragments of the mosaic (the disparate four tales) swirl into
place."20   By the end of the novel, José has attained order
and his own psychic equilibrium over chaos.   Lezama encourages his readers to "see life in its totality";21 a "true
freedom involves the control of one's own inner passions"22
and a continual search for "an adequate expression of their
creative impulse and their integration within life is seen as
a celebration of the creative act."23

   Paradiso is a highly imaginative work that plunges
somewhat headlong out of control of its novelistic structure,
which is responsible for its being characterized as "baroque"
and "hermetic."   Nevertheless, it is a highly experimental
work, seeking to impose order over chaos without stultifying
the creative impulse; it relies heavily upon the reader's collaboration within the creative process.

   In a delightful and fascinating paper Arthur J.
Sabatini tried to penetrate the creative act of Lezama Lima
by discussing three levels of allusions found in the vast and
intricate Paradiso, leaving innumerable interpretations open
to the reader.24   Utilizing Tzvetan Todorov's premise of
dismantling the text and relating each element to that text,
Sabatini whizzes through the abundant ancient, esoteric, and
hermetic allusions in Paradiso in order to determine a hierarchical relationship and signification summed up by the
phrase, "culture in the tropics."   He discovers the inciden-
tal, polemical and allusional series of images corresponding
to José Cemí's growth and awareness, and concludes that
Paradiso is an overwhelming creative work open to infinite
speculation.   It defies the critic: "Any analytic or descrip-
tive attempt is bound to be insufficient, because the novel
can be read at countless levels and in a myriad of ways."25
Emir Rodríguez Monegal feels that Lezama mixes

> a Rabelaisian sense of humor, highly convoluted
> prose with faulty scholarship, a wild imagination
> with the most ambitious re-thinking of the West's
> greatest works of literature and philosophy, pro-
> ducing a truly encyclopedic novel ... Lezama's
> one book, a condensation and expansion simultane-
> ously of everything he attempted previously. [26]

Indeed, the entire novel may be viewed as a kind of structured and baroque poem, [27] "a complex, thickly metaphorical
novel--[with] mannered Gongoristic syntax ... [an] intricate
verbal labyrinth. "[28]

The adjective that best describes Lezama Lima's
novel is ambitious.   Vargas Llosa called it "an impossible
attempt ... to totalize and codify his poetic system ... a
lofty and definitive Summa that would show in all its complexity ... his conceptions of art and of human life. "[29]
Part of the impossibility in reading Lezama is laid at the
door of his Cuban nationality.   He is a tropical writer, gar-
rulous and known for verbal excess that "has led to a kind
of apotheosis, a defect now becoming a virtue. "[30]   His
verbal universe is so dense that, as Julio Cortázar has
pointed out, Paradiso's complexity is closer to that of a
forest, or to a dionysiac ritual, than to the deliberate
structure of a cathedral.   Octavio Paz wrote that "Lezama
Lima's baroque is a verbal world that is fixed, like a
stalacite--time fixed in a glance, a stalacite fixed in poetic
adventure. "[31]

Paradiso is a "monstrous" work, unclassifiable, exhausting, demanding, exotic, visceral, eccentric, imaginative, a Bildungsroman of great latitude, dizzying, circular,
prurient, puritan, pleasing, encyclopedic, intricate, autobiographical, fragmented, orphic, androgynous, fantastic,
violent, marvelous, dazzling, graphic, baroque, brilliant,
mystifying, befuddling--in short, beyond description.

The book has its critics.   J. M. Alonso has characterized it as "distended" and Lezama Lima's prose style
as "heavily cosmetized ornateness. "[32]   Other qualities, such
as "ornamental erudition, " "vulgar snobbery, " "hierarchical
view of the world, " "artificial paradise, " "unremitting pro-
vincialism, " and "murkiness" are criticisms frequently
leveled at Lezama's prose.   Alonso: "Lezama himself is
neither convincing as a Realist nor as a Decandentist and
his use of Gongorist cultivation as a social status symbol

while remaining essentially within a Realist intent strikes me as a perversion of two perfectly noble traditions which is condemned to being without the virtues of either."33

This reader, however, tends to plunge headlong into Lezama's sprawling forest of metaphors and become immersed in Lezama's labyrinth.   One must submerge oneself in his novel, exasperating and inexhaustible as it is.   For Paradiso is controversial, the work of an expanding imagination, a linguistic tour de force of brilliant descriptions and poetic evocations, an outstanding example of the neo-Baroque element of Latin American literature and, most assuredly, a masterpiece of fiction.

4. GARCIA MARQUEZ: A NEW COLOMBIAN COSMOLOGY

In 1967 the appearance of Gabriel García Márquez's One
Hundred Years of Solitude was regarded as the most phen-
omenal literary event to have ever taken place in Latin
America. It made García Márquez an international over-
night sensation and injected the faltering reputation of the
Latin American novel with the highest prestige it had ever
been accorded. In fact, Pablo Neruda, the Nobel Prize-
winning poet, called its appearance "the greatest revolution
in the Spanish language since the Don Quixote of Cervantes."
Gabriel García Márquez and One Hundred Years of Solitude
created the new "boom" in Latin American literature; according to Mario Vargas Llosa, One Hundred Years provoked
a literary earthquake throughout Latin America. Critics
universally recognized the novel as a masterpiece of the art
of fiction, and the public endorsed this opinion, systematical-
ly exhausting new editions, which, at one point, appeared at
the outstanding rate of one per week. [1]   García Márquez, a
Colombian journalist and world traveler who now lives in
Mexico, has become as popular as Pelé. When One Hundred Years of Solitude went into international translation his
personal popularity and that of the novel were equally enthusiastic. "What is especially remarkable is that its thunder-
ing force should be due to virtues which can be defined as
artistic. "[2]

Like the other writers considered in this volume,
García Márquez is a nomad, a self-proclaimed exile who
generally became identified with the "boom" in Latin American literature and more widely known because of it. These
mainly younger writers broke with the past and sought their
own innovative narrative techniques. They became experimentalists, inventive in their language, cosmopolitan and

34

universal in the treatment of their themes. National boundaries could no longer contain them. García Márquez began
searching for his own national identity in Mexico, although
the social and moral issues he writes about are distinctly
Colombian.

Gabriel García Márquez was born on March 6, 1928,
in the dirty northern village of Aracataca, Colombia, a
small, remote locale near Barranquilla on the Caribbean
coast. He is the eldest of twelve children of Gabriel Eligio
García, a telegraph operator, and his wife María Márquez
Iguarán. He spent the first eight years of his life with his
maternal grandparents, Nicolas Márquez Iguarán and Tran-
quila Iguarán Cotes, since his parents lived in virtual poverty
in the coastal town of Ríohacha. García Márquez's grandparents lived in a great, gloomy house, thronged with relatives and memories, not far from a banana finca or planta-
tion called Macondo. His childhood impressions of
Aracataca's isolation, heat, and decay combined with the
stories he heard from his grandparents to give birth in his
imagination to the mythical town of Macondo, the setting of
most of his major fictions.

In 1936 García Márquez's parents moved further in-
land to the small town of Sucre, in the tropical grasslands,
and young Gabriel was sent to school first in Barranquilla
and later, after winning a scholarship at age eight, to the
National Colegio at Ziapaquira, a Jesuit-run school near
Bogotá, where he read the works of Jules Verne and Emilio
Salgari. In 1946 he received his bachillerato, and the following year he entered the National University of Colombia
in Bogotá, pursuing a law degree. The year 1947 was
crucial in García Márquez's life; he wrote and published
his first short story, "The Third Resignation," in the newspaper El Espectador, proving to a Colombian critic that
there were some Colombian writers who were not insignifi-
cant. The year 1948 was also significant for all Colombians:
after the assassination of Liberal leader Jorge Eljecer Gaitan
began la violencia, a state of siege akin to a civil war, which
lasted over ten years and cost hundreds of thousands of lives.
The university was closed that year, and García Márquez
moved with his parents to the port city of Cartagena. Ma-
triculating in the university there to continue his law studies, García Márquez also took a job as a journalist for the
newly established newspaper El Universal while continuing
to write some ten to fifteen short stories.

In 1950 he returned to Barranquilla, abandoning his

law studies and job with the newspaper to write a column
for El Heraldo. While working at this low-paying job, he
read voraciously and began work on his first novel, which
was published as Leaf Storm in 1955. [3] In 1954 he returned
to Bogotá and worked for El Espectador as a reporter and
film critic, writing short stories in his spare time. In 1955
he achieved celebrity status in Colombia by winning a prize
for imaginative fiction sponsored by the Association of Artists and Writers in Bogotá for his short story "The Day
After Sunday. " He also wrote a factual journalistic account
of the wreck of a Colombian naval destroyer, "Story of a
Shipwreck. " Told to him by the sole survivor, Luis
Alejandro Velasco, the story embarrassed the Rojas Pinilla
dictatorship and caused a political scandal: the boat had not
been sunk by a storm but by contraband cargo smuggled from
the United States that was incompetently stored on its deck.
García Márquez's exposé of the incident so increased the
sales of El Espectador that the newspaper made him their
roving European correspondent. After joining a cell of the
illegal Communist Party, García Márquez left Colombia for
the first time to cover the Big Four Conference in Geneva.
Spending several months in Rome, he took courses at the
Center for Experimental Cinematography. Learning that the
Rojas Pinilla dictatorship had closed down El Espectador because of the furor his story on Velasco caused, García
Márquez was suddenly without work or income.

          In 1956 he moved to Paris and spent two to three
years in a garret in virtual poverty while writing two short
novels, The Evil Hour (1957) and No One Writes to the
Colonel (1958). After finishing Colonel in 1957, García
Márquez toured East Germany, Czechoslovakia, Poland,
Russia, and Hungary. He moved to London and lived there
for two years before moving to Caracas to accept a job as
editor of the magazine Momento. Continuing his nomadic
existence, in 1958 he returned to Colombia to marry Mer-
cedes Barcha Prado, whom he had met in Sucre in 1950.
The year 1958 proved to be splendidly productive for García
Márquez: he and his new bride returned to Caracas, where
he worked for the magazine Momento and the gossip sheet
Venezuela Gráfica, and on his own collection of short stories,
Big Mama's Funeral (which was published in 1961). In 1959
García Márquez embraced the Cuban Revolution, worked for
Fidel Castro's news agency Prensa Latina in Colombia and
Havana, and became its assistant bureau chief in 1961. His
first son Rodrigo was born in 1959, and the following year
he returned to Cuba. Itinerant as ever, in 1961 García

Márquez worked in New York as second in command of
Castro's Prensa Latina; made his way by Greyhound bus
from New York to New Orleans; and embraced William
Faulkner's South (with the author's books under his arm)
enroute to Mexico, where he began a new career as screen-
writer and collaborator for a short time with Carlos Fuentes,
while eking out an income as a part-time journalist and pub-
licist.

While in Mexico García Márquez wrote another short
story, "The Sea of Lost Time," and took a job as editor of
the woman's magazine La familia and of Sucesos, a newspaper devoted to crime coverage and other sensational
events.   In 1961 The Evil Hour won the $3,000 Esso Liter-
ary Prize in Bogotá.   His second son, Gonzalo, was born
in 1962.   It was in this year that he decided to settle permanently in Mexico; he was going through a period of severe
self-criticism and dissatisfaction with his work: he wrote
no fiction for nearly five years.   In 1963 he resigned from
La familia and Sucesos to take a public-relations job with
the Walter Thompson Publicity Agency.   He began writing
his first film script with Carlos Fuentes, Time to Die,
which he completed by 1964.   In 1965 he finished another
script, H. O., filmed by Arturo Ripstein.   It was in this
crucial year, on an auto trip from Mexico City to Acapulco,
that the idea for One Hundred Years of Solitude occurred to
him.

García Márquez, his wife, and his sons lived in
Mexico City largely on borrowed money for the eighteen
months it took him to complete his longest novel.   Shutting
himself up for eight hours a day, he finally completed the
novel he had been trying to write since his adolescence.
"It was so complete in my mind that I could have read,
right then and there, the first chapter of it into a dicto-
phone."[4]   Parts of One Hundred Years began to appear in
periodicals all over the world; the entire novel was finally
published in Buenos Aires in 1967.

In 1967 García Márquez attended the thirteenth Inter-
national Congress for Ibero-American Literature in Caracas
and won the Rómulo Gallegos Prize.   He also won the
Primera Plana Prize in Buenos Aires the same year and
moved to Barcelona, Spain, with his family.   One Hundred
Years of Solitude became a literary sensation, winning the
French Prize for the Best Foreign Book and the Italian
Prize, and was chosen one of the best twelve books by
United States literary critics in 1970.

Towards the end of the 1960s García Márquez returned to the short story, producing in 1968 "A Very Old Man with Enormous Wings, " "The Handsomest Drowned Man in the World, " "The Last Voyage of the Ghost Ship, " and "Blacaman the Good, Vendor of Miracles. " His career is now gliding chiefly on the fame of One Hundred Years. In 1968 he first met Mario Vargas Llosa; they jointly published The Novel in Latin America: A Dialogue. Vargas Llosa was to write, in 1977, the first comprehensive full-length study of García Márquez's works, García Márquez: Story of a Deicide. It was also in 1968 that García Márquez began to write The Autumn of the Patriarch, inspired by the fall of Marcos Pérez Jiménez of Venezuela, "an incredible old man walking through the huge, abandoned rooms of a palace full of animals. "5   Probably influenced by the life of Venezuelan caudillo Juan Vicente Gómez, life under the dictatorship of Rojas Pinilla in Colombia, Castro's Cuban takeover, Franco's death (as well as Caesar's and Mussolini's), the wife-worship of Perón, Strössner's durable regime, and Trujillo's relations with the United States, García Márquez finished the novel in 1971, continued to embellish it, and published it in Spain in 1975, after "absorbing and re-imagining all this and more, and emerged with a stunning portrait of the archetype: the pathological fascist tyrant. "6

In the 1970s García Márquez continued writing short stories; the collections The Incredible Sad Tale of Innocent Eréndira and Her Heartless Grandmother, Blue-dog Eyes, and The Black Who Made the Angels Wait were all published in 1972, although the author would have preferred not to have the last two collections published.   Becoming one of the most celebrated spokespeople for the new Latin American novel, he won the Rómulo Gallegos Prize again in 1972 in Caracas (he donated the proceeds to a small left-wing group, the Movement Towards Socialism) and accepted the $10, 000 Books Abroad/Neustadt International Prize for Literature.   Books Abroad dedicated an entire issue to his life and career in 1973, as Review, published by the Center for Inter-American Relations, had devoted an entire issue to One Hundred Years of Solitude in 1970.   In 1973 García Márquez published When I Was Happy and Undocumented, a collection of his journalistic pieces.   He also traveled to Norman, Oklahoma, to collect the Books Abroad Prize and began work on a major new novel centering on an almost-immortal Latin American dictator, completing the first draft.

After traveling in Spain, France, and Mexico, García

Márquez in 1974 founded a news magazine, Alternativa, in Bogotá. In the following year The Autumn of the Patriarch, his second novel, appeared. Also in 1975 he published All the Short Stories of Gabriel García Márquez (1947-72) and left Barcelona with the intention of living in Mexico and Colombia. Over the past four years various translations into English of his short stories and major novels (Autumn appeared here in English in 1975) have been published.

García Márquez still works and resides in Mexico with his wife and two sons. In 1976 Columbia University in New York awarded him an honorary Doctorate of Letters. A dark, curly-haired, stout man with a huge Pancho Villa-type mustache, García Márquez's chief recreation is listening to recorded music with a passionate and obsessive intensity worthy of one of his own eccentric character creations. 7

In July of 1978 García Márquez, passing through New York on his way home to Mexico, joked about his immigrant status. Like Julio Cortázar and Carlos Fuentes among others, he is on a "blacklist" known to immigration authorities because he belongs to subversive organizations. Subject to special visa restrictions, he can only enter the United States when invited by a particular university to lecture. In 1978 he spent some time "lecturing" at Columbia University and discussed his own work, and that of Borges and Somerset Maugham. His celebrity status even affected the composition of The Autumn of the Patriarch. Because of his own prominence, García Márquez realized the nature of the "power" his celebrity status brought him. At the outset of the Castro revolution his attendance at the trials of Batista supporters, where he listened to many monologues of the fallen generals and police officials, inspired him with a new narrative device for Autumn: the multiple monologue--many voices telling the same story. He has even declared Autumn was a more interesting book to work on technically than One Hundred Years.

At present, like Alejo Carpentier, he is working on a book about the Cuban revolution and how it has affected the Cubans' lives, using Daniel Defoe's A Journal of the Plague Year as a model. In addition to writing some short stories, he is also working on a semidocumentary film with Costa-Gavras, the Paris-based Greek director of extraordinary political films such as Z and State of Siege, and is planning to write his memoirs with the object of "telling the real stories behind One Hundred Years of Solitude. "8

If One Hundred Years of Solitude (1967) is García Márquez's acknowledged masterpiece, then everything he wrote subsequently must fall far from the mark of expert craftsmanship.   True, The Autumn of the Patriarch is not as universally embraced as One Hundred Years, nor has it received the avalanche of critical exposure that greeted its predecessor.   And because it took time to separate itself from the powerful shadow of the earlier book, most readers, wanting to return to the glorious world of Macondo, viewed it as a disappointment.   Also because the book was a long time in writing and was promised long before it arrived, it created more disappointment among readers and reviewers than it rightfully deserved and was accorded less critical space than any of García Márquez's subsequent fictions. Nevertheless, The Autumn of the Patriarch is a finely honed novel, even superior to Solitude, and is a book that requires a very attentive first reading because of its extraordinary stylistic techniques.   It represents García Márquez's fusion of all literary influences on his work, especially William Faulkner, James Joyce, and Virginia Woolf (which he readily acknowledges) merged into a single, unified stream of prose.

The Autumn of the Patriarch is a devastating portrait of a Latin American dictator, reminiscent of the Guatemalan Miguel Angel Asturias's brilliant El Señor Presidente but written in an extraordinary "stream of consciousness style revealing the hollow rhetoric, fragility and fearful insecurity of the tyrant's reign."[9]   It is the story of the life of an imaginary but archetypal dictator as seen through the lens of "magic realism."   Reflecting on Solitude, the book's translator, Gregory Rabassa, has this comment to offer that also applies to the style of Autumn:

> This trait of his writing (doing what is exactly right and not thinking about it) always rings true that it seems to have a touch of magic about it, so real, hence "magical realism."   He has introduced in a natural or objective manner improbable or miraculous events in a basically realistic narrative.   But it is not just that: it is reality in its several dimensions, the ones we are hard put to explain without recourse to naked formulas.   He has returned to the roots of reality, which are the roots of the novel as it was conceived by Cervantes. But he has gone even deeper and given us the Roc once more.   That is the nature of his ancient art.[10]

García Márquez has organized the book into six episodes of varying length, circular narratives, each beginning
at the point of the patriarch's death. Within these narrative
divisions the story of the patriarch's rise to power is re-
counted largely in his own mind in fragmentary fashion. The
narrative flows back and forth in time, creating a chronological jumble, what one critic called "a densely rich and fluid
pudding that makes Faulknerian leaps forward and backward
in time, making the novel a puzzle of pronouns, consistently
changing narrative points of view in mid-sentence."11 The
novel uses a stream-of-consciousness technique that defies
strict chronology. <u>Autumn</u> begins at the end of the general's
life and takes us through a whirlpool of events. We are
drawn into the vortex of obsessional images of brutal power
and the fear of death, vultures picking at the corpse, a palm
in ruins in a

> Joycean delirium of language and associations.
> The novel proceeds to swirl around and through
> the megalomania of power, the strategies, the
> brutalities, the myths, the hysteria of his time-
> less reign of gloom ... creating an intensely sug-
> gestive structure of memories.12

Each chapter or division encompasses two or three crucial
episodes in the dictator's career and introduces one or two
important characters in his life. Our patriarch is never
named, and there are only a few characters that are fully
represented.

The first section deals with his double, Patricio
Aragones, and his eventual death. The second presents the
patriarch's rise to power, his relationship with the beauty
queen Manuela Sánchez, and their mysterious disappearance
timed with the eclipse of the sun. In the third section we
witness the general's strategies for power, floods, and the
death of his right-hand man and Chief of National Security
General Rodrigo de Aguilar. The fourth section is concerned with the death of Benedición Alvarado, his mother,
a former bird vendor and prostitute, her canonization, and
the appearance of Leticia Nazareno, his future wife. The
fifth section describes the patriarch's marriage, the death
of his wife and his son Emmanual--who are both torn to bits
in a public marketplace by trained dogs--and introduces
Ignacio Saenz de la Barra, a sadist who is hired to seek out
the murderers of the patriarch's family as the latter cele-
brates the hundredth anniversary of his reign. The sixth and

last section narrates the patriarch's extreme solitude and
his physical decay and recounts his death once more.

All of the characters and events in this wild, incred-
ibly exaggerated, and hallucinogenic novel are told in an atmosphere where the "debris of despotism phosphoresces with
decay and the vultures in charge of that palace cleanup are
history's ageless witnesses."[13]   The novel is also seasoned
with surrealistic details that exaggerate the general's power
as described by the unidentified multiple narrators and give
it a tone of magical realism.   For example, our protagonist
has the power to change the hour of the day; arrange eclipses
of the sun; sell the Caribbean Sea to the United States and
transport it piece by piece to Arizona; and literally stuff,
sew up, and roast the treacherous Rodrigo de Aguilar, serving him as a meal to his fellow officers.   Other outrageous
qualities the patriarch possesses are the following: an en-
larged testicle (the source of his masochism), which although
it pains him throughout his life helps him to bear five thousand
children during his 232-year life; a third set of teeth cut at
age 150; an ability to converse with all kinds of animals and
cure all kinds of diseases with salt and even predict the
future.

The astonishing, amusing absurdities and images
create a cumulative dazzling effect of phantasmagorical
lyricism.   What García Márquez is actually exposing, as
his narrative moves back, forth, and laterally, is the
governmental chaos of his own native Colombia, although,
for that matter, his views could be applied to any country
or South American dictatorship.   According to Alastair Reid,

> The Autumn of the Patriarch is bound to be com-
> pared with Miguel Angel Asturias' El Señor Presi-
> dente.   But Asturias' novel is more concerned with
> dictatorship as an evil and his ironies are savage.
> García Márquez is more concerned with dictator-
> ships as myth in the popular mind.[14]

If Autumn is a diatribe against dictatorship, it is still one
of the most highly stylized "mystical, surrealistic, Rabelaisi-
an [books] in its excesses, its distortion and its exotic
language."[15]   Although some of García Márquez's writing
can run on without punctuation for fifty-three pages or so,
here is a shorter example of his unique prose style that
sets the tone of the entire novel:

The first time they found him had been at the

beginning of his autumn, the nation was still lively
enough for him to feel menaced by death even in
the solitude of his bedroom, and still he governed
as if he knew he was predestined never to die, for
at that time it did not look like a presidential palace but rather a marketplace where a person had
to make his way through barefoot orderlies unload-
ing vegetables and chicken cages from donkeys in
the corridors, stepping over beggar women with
famished godchildren who were sleeping in a huddle
on the stairs awaiting the miracle of official char-
ity, it was necessary to elude the flow of dirty
water from the foul-mouthed concubines who were
putting fresh flowers in the vases in the place of
nocturnal flowers and swabbing the floor and sing-
ing songs of illusory loves to the rhythm of the
dry branches that beat rugs on the balconies and
all of it in the midst of the uproar of tenured civil
servants who found hens laying eggs in desk
drawers, and, the traffic of whores and soldiers
in the toilets, and a tumult of birds, and the fighting of street dogs in the midst of audiences because no one knew who was who or by whom in
that palace with open doors in the grand disorder
of which it was impossible to locate the government (pp. 6-7).

As each section progresses, the sentences become longer
and longer, creating a spiraling effect that "adds up to a
boiling cauldron of rage, lament, sarcasm, despair, affection, hope and exasperation."[16] In the only fairly complete
book of criticism published in English on García Márquez's
life and work, George R. McMurray has some interesting
thoughts on Autumn's style:

> The numerous narrative voices would seem to func-
> tion as the writer's multiple, lyrical self, while
> the lengthy rambling sentences weave a tightly knit
> fabric of motifs intended to illustrate momentary
> states of mind rather than to develop characters
> in the traditional sense.... The plot appears to
> be molded by contrapuntal images, a narrative
> technique that substitutes perception for action....[17]

Perhaps McMurray's most beautifully expressed statement to
describe Autumn is the following: "The Autumn of the Patriarch can be [best] described as a fluid montage of illuminated moments."[18]

Autumn is a work of excesses, of immensity, dense and enormous, just as life itself is enormous.   And although Autumn "has none of the life-celebrating quality that made One Hundred Years of Solitude so universally embraced, ... it is a supreme polemic, a spiritual exposé, an attack against any society that encourages or even permits the growth of such a monstrosity."[19]

García Márquez has come a bit farther stylistically, although the theme of Autumn is virtually the same as that of One Hundred Years--solitude, the solitude of absolute power.   The patriarch is himself a victim of the false sense of power he created.   García Márquez "is obsessed with the problem of the substance of the isolated imagination, intoxicated by itself."[20]   The Autumn of the Patriarch, like One Hundred Years, is a novel of excesses.   It is extraordinarily gross, lecherous, savage, and grotesque in its intrigues. For García Márquez believes in depicting in his novels the immensity that exists in life.   For him, "life is enormous, dense and mysterious"[21] and always a celebration.

García Márquez's oeuvre has always been "illuminated by the transformations his imagination is capable of making, the humanity of his perception, his accurate astonishment, even on a small scale, in a phrase or minor incident."[22] Autumn possesses a rich artistic vision.   García Márquez genuinely succeeds in destroying the line that separates reality from the fantastic and reduces the marvelous to daily experience, which allows him "to create characters, some revolutionary, some cruel, some tender, some fantastic and a number who dream dreams in a tropical climate of brooding solitude and poetic nostalgia."[23]

There are, however, several dissenting opinions about Autumn that are noteworthy.   A certain slack monotony sets into the prose because it "lacks the energy of a full stop."[24]   Usually compared to its predecessor, Autumn was considered by some critics "a heartbreaking disappointment ... static and suffocating, in its oversumptuousness[25] unendingly bizarre and forward but ultimately, not difficult."[26] George R. McMurray suggested that the author cut at least twenty-five pages from the last, "tedious," section and commented unfavorably on García Márquez's extremely long sentence structure with its numerous repetitions; the lack of tension between poetry and horror at the novel's conclusion, due to the introduction of a first-person soliloquy; and the general lack of lyricism, which McMurray attributed to

García Márquez's Faulknerian prose.[27]   Because Autumn
uses hyperbole as its chief stylistic resource, Emir Rodríguez Monegal believed that the novel "suffers from its concentration on one single, predictable character"; it becomes
"tedious and despite some brilliant episodes, fails to hold
the reader's interest."[28]   He warned García Márquez to re-
think carefully his future course as novelist.   Autumn was
also viewed as "Beckettian in rhythm yet full of all the stuff
that Beckett leaves out, Nabokovian in its appetizing abundance yet quite without his mincing, dandyistic sheen."[29]
Paul West believed, somewhat differently, that Autumn, ultimately, had "no message, no interpretation, no answers
but only a chance to catalogue what the senses find and cannot do without,"[30] a phenomenological view attesting perhaps
to García Márquez's narrative kinesis of an empty-headed
perception of reality, leaving us with an effect of "marmore-
al amplitute, precision-studded vagueness, with volcanos of
Proustian saliences"[31] but empty harvests for its readers.

Yet Autumn is an astounding work.   Its patriarch
may be the author's most memorable literary creation, and
"García Márquez's most brilliantly stylized portrait ... is
likely to stretch his reader's imagination to the limit."[32]
Bernard Malamud felt that Autumn "depicted the world's
madnesses [with] a terrible irony, unrelenting as Swift's
Gulliver's Travels, brilliantly interwoven with wild poetic
images of decay."[33]

The Autumn of the Patriarch continues to excite controversy.   As a spirally constructed collage, it is "not only
the most original Latin American novel to date on the timely subject of political tyranny, but also an ingenious experiment in prose fiction."[34]   After reading it, one can easily
see why Gabriel García Márquez is one of the best-known
self-exiled novelists from Latin America and perhaps the
most gifted, innovative, and creative writer of his generation.

5. VARGAS LLOSA: THE PERUVIAN EXPERIENCE

The author of the definitive analysis of Gabriel García
Márquez's literary works, Mario Vargas Llosa is internationally known as a major novelist in his own right.   Born
in Arequipa, Peru, on March 8, 1936, Jorge Mario Pedro
Vargas Llosa, an only child, spent most of his childhood in
the very old and traditional city of Cochabamba, Bolivia,
with his divorced mother and paternal grandparents.   From
1937 to 1945 he attended the LaSalle School in Cochabamba;
he became a spoiled child, involved only in his own fanta-
sies.   His parents had separated two months before he was
born.   His father worked for an airline in Lima before his
mother returned to Arequipa.   In 1945 Vargas Llosa returned to Peru, to Piura--which became the setting for his
second novel, The Green House--and spent a horrible year
in this desert city.   The following year, when his father,
Ernesto Vargas, reunited with his mother, Dora Llosa,
young Mario attended the Salesino School, where he had difficulty adjusting to his classmates.   Shortly thereafter Vargas Llosa moved to Lima with his parents, and from 1950
to 1952 he became a boarding-school student at the Leoncio
Prado Military Academy, the setting of his first novel, A
Time of the Hero.   He had applied to the Naval Academy
but was rejected because he did not meet the proper age re-
quirement.   Leoncio Prado was part school, part reforma-
tory and military academy, an excellent setting for difficult
adolescent boys.   Mario suffered from maladjustment, anxiety, and restlessness.   Reading became an outlet for his own
revolt against the academy.   He graduated in two years--one
year less than the three usually required--and in 1952 returned to Piura to complete his last year of high school at
the San Miguel School.   While there he led a strike against
the head of the institution, which became the theme for the

short story "The Bosses." As a student, he also worked as a part-time editor and columnist for the newspaper La Industria and saw his only play, Escape of the Inca, produced in Piura's Teatro Variedades.

Returning to Lima in 1953, Vargas Llosa attended the University of San Marcos, studied law and obtained his bachillerato in 1957. On a scholarship he also attended the University of Madrid, where he eventually obtained a Doctorate in Literature in 1971. At age nineteen he caused a family scandal by marrying a Bolivian woman, Julia Urquidi; they were divorced a few years later. Also in 1958 Vargas Llosa published his first book, a group of five short stories entitled The Bosses, which won the Leopoldo Alas Literary Prize in Spain. The book showed deep insight into adolescent psychoanalysis, especially the behavior and language of teenagers. The Bosses contains the key to many of the major themes that Vargas Llosa explores in his subsequent novels, which are usually considered social and political indictments of his native Peru. At about this time, he edited the magazine Literatura, wrote many articles for other newspapers and magazines, such as Mercurio Persiano, and became a journalist.

In 1958 Vargas Llosa took his first trip to Paris, to collect a prize sponsored by the Revue Française for a short story, "The Challenge." He returned to Peru, making his first trip as journalist through the dense jungles of the region of the upper Marañón River (which was to become the setting for The Green House) and published an account of his trip. In 1959 Vargas Llosa returned to Paris, where he taught Spanish at the Berlitz School, did clerical work for the Agence France Presse, and organized for the French Radio-TV Network a series of short-wave radio broadcasts to South America. It was in France, where he lived until 1966, that his life as an exile truly begins. In an interview in 1967 Vargas Llosa maintained that his distance from Peru was purely a "physical" one, because Peru had been his only subject even when he was living elsewhere. During this period he came to meet many other Latin American exiled writers--Cortázar, Carpentier, Angel Asturias, Borges, and Fuentes--and concentrated on writing his first novel, A Time of the Hero, which was published in Barcelona in 1962, after a year's delay due to censorship difficulties.

Winning the Biblioteca Breve Prize for 1962 and the Critics Prize for 1963 (and missing the prestigious Formen-

tor Prize by one vote), A Time of the Hero launched Vargas
Llosa's international literary career: it became an instant
best-seller and was translated into twenty languages.   Considered Vargas Llosa's first tour de force, the book also
created a scandal in the Leoncio Prado Military Academy
and aroused such public indignation that one thousand copies
of the book were burned there by less appreciative Peruvians.

In 1964 Vargas Llosa returned to Peru for a brief
period, traveling into the jungle for a second time, studying
the settings for a future book.   He underwent a marital
crisis and divorce.   One year later he traveled to Havana,
serving as a judge for the literary prizes awarded by the
magazine Casa de las Américas, the first of several excursions where Vargas Llosa proclaimed his true belief in the
principles of Castro's Cuban revolution (and a few years
later, his eventual disappointment with Cuban Communism).
Also in May of 1965 he married his first cousin Patricia
Llosa on a return trip to Lima.

In 1966 The Green House was published after three
revisions, the result of his trips into the Peruvian jungle.
Another complex novel, critical of the Peruvian government,
it earned him the Critic's Prize for 1966, Peru's National
Novel Prize, and in 1967 the prestigious Rómulo Gallegos
International Prize.   The year 1966 was a critical year for
Vargas Llosa: he was invited for the first time to New York
City by the P. E. N. Club.   He also lectured and became a
jury member for various awards in Buenos Aires and Monte-
video.   Near the end of the year he moved to London (Ken-
sington), where he lectured at Queen Mary College of the
University of London while writing for magazines and news-
papers.   On a short return trip to Lima his first son,
Alvaro, was born.

In 1967 Vargas Llosa's first novella, The Young Pups,
was published.   It was later made into a sensational film,
although it was never shown in the United States.   Dealing
with the activities of upper- and middle-class adolescents in
Lima's suburbs, it was considered a send-up of the evils
caused by the Latin American ideal of machismo.   He also
penned an important prologue to the complete works of
Sebastián Salázar Bondy, defining the vocation of a writer.
Also at this time his second son, Gonzalo, was born in
Lima.

In 1968 Vargas Llosa became a writer-in-residence at

the University of Washington.   Previous to taking this post,
he received many international invitations, traveling with his
family to Finland, Sweden, Czechoslovakia, Italy, and the
U. S. S. R.   Once settled in Washington, he embarked upon
composing his longest novel to date, Conversations in the
Cathedral, published the following year.   Once again, his
theme was Peru during the Manuel Odría dictatorship of
1948-63, exposing government hypocrisy and corruption
through "conversations" that take place in a sleazy river-
side bar ironically called "The Cathedral. "

     In 1969 Vargas Llosa became Visiting Professor at
the University of Puerto Rico in Rio Piedras; one year later
he took up residence in Barcelona, Spain, working on History
of a Deicide, his critical literary history of Gabriel García
Márquez, which was published there in 1971 (a portion was
submitted as his doctoral dissertation at the University of
Madrid).   It is coincidental, but perhaps not so strange, that
Vargas Llosa's writing style, nomadic life, and career so
closely resemble that of García Márquez.   Applying critical
analysis to his own novels, Vargas Llosa wrote his own absorbing critical study of the art of fiction, Secret History of
a Novel (1972), which tells how his third novel, The Green
House, came to be written.

     Continually dividing his time between writing his own
fiction and literary criticism, Vargas Llosa's fourth novel,
for which he also wrote the screenplay, was published in an
edition of one hundred thousand copies--Captain Pantoja and
the Special Service (1973).   In 1974 another critical work,
The Perpetual Orgy: Gustave Flaubert and Mme. Bovary,
was published.   Pantoja, the subject of this chapter, is
Vargas Llosa's first venture into social criticism by way of
humor: in it he takes a mordant look at two Peruvian insti-
tutions: the army and organized religion.   It is one of his
shortest and most successfully translated novels, and appeared recently in the United States to enormous critical
acclaim.   The year 1974 was a special one for the author:
his daughter Morgana was born, and the entire family returned to Lima from self-imposed exile.

     Among his critical writings, Vargas Llosa's "Litera-
ture Is Fire" speech, presented on August 4, 1967, in
Caracas, is well known, since it defines the mission of
most Latin American writers at the full peak of the "boom"
as well as his own nonconformism.   It was in Caracas that
he first met García Márquez, marking the beginning of a

very close friendship that subsequently ended in a melee in
Mexico City several years later. "The Novel in Latin America: A Dialogue" (1968) was the transcription of a conversation he had with his idol, García Márquez, in Lima about
the genesis of the latter's One Hundred Years of Solitude.
An Imaginary Combat (1971), written with the collaboration
of Martin Riquer, is a series of essays on the French
chivalric novel Tirant lo Blanch. In fiction, Vargas Llosa's
short story "Sunday" was published in Buenos Aires in 1976;
another novel, Aunt Julia and the Writer (1977), begun in
1975 and supposedly inspired by a radio broadcast he heard
during his youth, has yet to appear here in English.

During 1977 Vargas Llosa returned briefly to the
United States and participated in a symposium at the University of Oklahoma dealing with his works. He was the President of the P. E. N. Club for 1979. At the time of this writing, he was living in Lima, after several years in literary
exile in Paris, Barcelona, and London. Vargas Llosa is
certainly one of Latin America's brightest, most intelligent,
and amusing young novelists. He has become politically
engagé since his return to Peru in 1975. As headlines in
the New York Times testify, he has emerged as the most
articulate critic of the left-wing military government:
"Famed Novelist Clashes with Peru's Military Rulers" (February 21, 1975); "Peruvian Novelist Turns Film Maker and
Tangles With the Army" (November 22, 1977); "Peru Novelist
Warns Against Military Nationalism" (February 15, 1979).
The second of these headlines is the most interesting from a
literary perspective, since it deals with the banning of a
film, produced by the author, based on Captain Pantoja and
the Special Service, in which Vargas Llosa himself also
played a small role.

Vargas Llosa most assuredly is a courageous writer
who continually champions a free exchange of ideas, a free
spirit of criticism, a free press, and an authentic culture.
Presently, he lives and works in Peru, and, unlike Julio
Cortázar, he continues writing fiction critical of Peruvian
society as a resident. No longer an exile, he is a citizen
participating in the evolution of Peru's changing society.

Mario Vargas Llosa is considered one of the most
"traditional" novelists in Latin American literature. His
perennial theme is the uses and abuses of power. If García
Márquez is considered the William Faulkner of Colombia,
Vargas Llosa's "naturalism" makes him the Theodore Dreiser

of Peru.   Vargas Llosa never tires of denouncing corruption,
violence, and injustice.   And he relies on traditional plots
and characterization while maintaining his role as a political
moralist. 1

Vargas Llosa originally planned Captain Pantoja and
the Special Service as a serious study, conceived as a dialogue.   After writing the first version, he felt that he had
penned a false, empty series of episodes.   However, when
he changed his perspective, from serious writing to humor,
the novel became a living entity.   He said of it: "It is the
first time I very much enjoyed writing a novel. "2   Former-
ly "allergic" to humor in fiction Vargas Llosa transformed
Pantoja into a hilarious book, in which he admittedly uses a
"brusque, direct kind of humor which permitted him to render more persuasively and truthfully several truculent and
absurd situations"3 in the novel.

Pantoja is the story of how an army officer,
Pantaleón Pantoja, organizes prostitution for the military in
the jungle outposts of Peru in the early 1950s.   Pantaleón
("a lion in all things"4) Pantoja creates, organizes, and
supplies a corps of visitadoras to provide sexual activity
and release for his troops near Iquitos, a remote army
military base.

The first chapter presents Panta, "a born organizer
with a methodological sense of order and executive capacity"
(p. 3) and Colonel Lopez Lopez giving the order to establish
a "special service" for the military with the greatest secre-
cy as a remedy for the sexual outrages against decent people
taking place near these remote military outposts.   We also
meet Pocha, his naive wife; her mother Leonor; a variety of
macho military types--Lieutenant Bracaconzo, Tiger Col-
lazos, Commander Beltrán; clergy, such as Father Francisco; and pimps, madams, and prostitutes, among them Chino,
Porfiro, and Madame Chuchupe.   Panta's real love is the
army.   He is obsessed with military orders and discipline,
a true maniac in his work.

Chapter Two is in three sections, two of which are
dispatches written by Pantoja, which hilariously detail the
statistical side of his special service: the potential number
of users, a sample questionnaire for the army, a report on
the range of services provided by prostitutes (with rates for
each), and the desire for green and red colors to lend

emblematic credence to his special service.   Another section, narrated by an omniscient author, describes the aspir-
ations of each of the novel's main characters on two particular evenings: Panta's anxiety for a new stripe, Pocha's need
for better living accommodations, Mother Leonor's desire to
keep home and hearth together, the military's desire for success of the extremely secret operation.

The third chapter consists of a long, rambling letter
written by Pocha to her sister Chichi, corroborating Panta's
new, very important "mission" with the Intelligence Service,
his fanatacism and enslavement to his work, her puzzlement
over Panta's visits to the local red-light districts, and her
attachment to Sinchi, the Voice of Radio Amazon, her favorite gossipy radio program.   In another short section narrated impressively by the author, we witness Pantoja's pain-
ful operation for hemorrhoids, his only consolation Dr.
Negrón's philosophy that everything that happens in life is
for the better.

The fourth chapter consists of eight separate confidential documents written in military jargon by Pantoja and
other officials detailing the establishment of the operation for
"special services":   an experiment using red porpoise oil to
increase sexual desire; use of the hydroplane Delilah for
transport; arranging for medical personnel to inspect the
prostitutes; use of a transport ship, the Eve, as a floating
"service" station; the introduction of four prostitutes, Lalita,
Iris, Knockers, and Sandra, and a time study made of their
servicing of twenty men; an accounting and financial statement of pay for services performed, detailed with deductions
for materials; a chaplain's letter to the Military Commander
condemning the use of prostitutes for the army and the Commander's reply condoning sexuality and asking the chaplain to
"close his eyes" to the situation.

Chapters Five, Six, and Seven describe the experiences of Pantoja's operation.   The fifth chapter is written
as a dialogue, beginning with the sentence "Wake up, Panta!,"
a circular refrain that begins the novel, reappears throughout
it, and closes the last chapter, clearly the salient leitmotif
urging Panta's spiritual awakening to Peru's corrupt military,
his enslavement to the army, his narrow-mindedness and
need for order superimposed from the ranks above, his lack
of individualism and responsibility.   In Chapter Five we meet
a total of ten prostitutes and a new girl called the "Brazilian"
who later becomes Pantoja's personal lover.   Vargas Llosa

introduces us to her in a humorous, delightfully parodic
style that is typical of the entire novel:

> "Delighted to see you again, Mr. Pantoja, " the
> Brazilian devours him with her eyes, wiggles,
> perfumes the air, chirps. "So this is the famous
> Pantiland. Really, I'd heard so much about it and
> I couldn't imagine what it'd be like. "
> "The famous what?" Pantaleón Pantoja pushes
> his head forward, brings up a chair. "Please sit
> down. "
> "Pantiland, that's what people call this, " the
> Brazilian spreads her arms, shows her shaved
> armpits, laughs. "Not only here in Iquitos, but
> everywhere. I heard of Pantiland in Manaos.
> What a funny name--does it come from Disney-
> land?"
> "I'm afraid it probably comes from Panta, "
> Mr. Pantoja looks her up and down, side to side,
> smiles at her, grows serious, smiles again, per-
> spires. "But you're Peruvian and not Brazilian,
> aren't you? At least in the way you speak. "
> "I was born here. They gave me that name
> because I lived in Manaos, " the Brazilian sits
> down, hikes her skirt, takes out her compact,
> powders her nose, the dimples in her cheeks.
> "But you see, everybody goes back to the country
> where he was born--just like in the song"
> (pp. 98-99).

Chapter Five also introduces Sinchi, the Voice of Radio
Amazon, who eventually causes the dismantling of the special service. Sinchi tries in vain to profit from the secret
operation, newly dubbed "Pantiland, " by blackmailing
Pantoja in exchange for radio silence. Meanwhile, Pocha
and her mother are learning, little by little, about the
Pantiland operation.

Chapter Six presents some sixteen documents, detailing the problems of expansion; guidelines for the selection
of users; statistical reports after the first year of opera-
tions; a satirical "Hymn of the Special Service, " sung by the
girls to the tune of the "Mexican Hat Dance" (a priceless
gag); chauvinist communiqués objecting to the use of "Mexican Hat Dance" rather than a Peruvian tune; radio messages
congratulating Pantoja on the birth of his daughter Gladys;
another blackmail threat from Sinchi in the form of an

unsigned letter; a letter documenting the marriage of
Maclovia, a prostitute to 1st Sgt. Teófilo Gualiano; requests
to increase the corps from twenty to thirty specialists; dispatches asking for changes in the lyrics of the hymn to include not just the army but other military branches as well;
a letter from Maclovia to Pocha; and finally a request for
an army discharge by a chaplain who cannot remain indifferent to procuring, a symptom of national decadence.

In Chapter Seven a radio exposé of Pantiland by the
Voice of Sinchi, complete with an eye-witness report from
Maclovia (who had been drummed out of the special service
because of her marriage), signifies the downfall of the operation.   Sinchi also has the audacity to ask Pocha for an
interview on the air, but Pocha leaves Loreto (Iquitos) with
her daughter.

In Chapter Eight, with Pocha gone, Pantoja consum-
mates his affair with an indifferent Brazilian, proving that
sex has no conscience in the tropics, and blames his job
for his new slavish attitude toward sexuality.   Panta characterizes his disease as "a sense of unhealthy obligation"
(p. 168).   Needless to say, after its exposure by Sinchi
the very creators and organizers desire an end to the special service.   But Panta is so proud of the success of his
work, he wants to continue the service, remaining as a
soldier-administrator.   Imagining himself as the "Einstein
of fucking" and "the great pimp of Peru," he envisages flying brigades of specialists in the most remote corners of
Peru, with groups of "exclusive" specialists for officers.
Even the officers of the service agree that the situation has
gotten out of hand.

Chapters Eight and Nine describe the downfall of the
service, the latter chapter through a series of newspaper
accounts detailing the death and crucifixion of the Brazilian
at Nauta by a group of men known as the "Brotherhood of
the Ark," who surreptiously boarded the Eve and raped the
specialists.   The Brazilian was killed in a crossfire between
the army and civilians.   Other articles in this chapter include a hilarious biography of the Brazilian, written in the
1940 movie-tabloid style of Photoplay magazine, detailing
her youth, affairs, and tragic end; an epistle to the "good"
concerning the "wicked" by Brother Francisco; an article
attesting to a police assault on a Loreto journalist, accusing
the former of abusing "freedom of the press"; and finally a
news item attesting that the seven civilians would not be
tried by a military tribunal.

The tenth and final chapter is a dialogue.   Three
years have passed since the inception of the service.   The
Brazilian's death is now viewed as that of a soldier fallen
in action.   General Scavino, who had been the lone dissenter
in creating the special service, blames Pantoja for trying to
make a fool of the army; the latter points out that all studies
have conclusively proved that since the founding of the special
service noncommissioned officers and soldiers tolerated life
in the jungle better.   General Scavino delivers the death
knell to the service.   Kaput.   Fini.   Pantoja, in disbelief,
collapses in tears.   The pimps and the prostitutes want to
continue the special service privately with Pantoja as its
captain, but the latter cannot bring himself to work outside
of a military context.

> "It's not that it makes me sad, " Pantita spends
> his last night in Iquitos wandering the deserted
> streets of Iquitos by himself and with his head
> down.   "After all, its three years of my life.
> They gave me a very difficult assignment and I
> executed it.   Despite the difficulties, the lack of
> understanding, I did good work.   I built something
> that had life, that was growing, that was useful.
> Now they destroy it with one blow and don't even
> thank me" (p. 235).

The Voice of Sinchi announces that Pantoja is sent
back to Lima, reunited with his wife, and reassigned to a
remote garrison at Pomata near Lake Titicaca, where the
army needs a new Quartermaster.   Panta is advised to keep
a low profile if he wants to remain in the army, so that
time will erase the stigma of his participation in the special
service.   In the last scene we see Panta awakened by his
wife to have breakfast at 5 A.M. in the remote mountain
outpost of Pomata, slavishly devoted to, once again, doing
his duty.

Captain Pantoja and the Special Service begins as a
traditional novel with an easily conceived narrative opening
its first chapter.   The dialogued chapters are the most interesting, although sometimes there is difficulty in separating
out one dialogue taking place simultaneously with another.
Despite the dazzling effects of chapters filled with mock
army documents, messages, and the like, Vargas Llosa is
a solid narrator and develops his characters in the round,
with a

sense of humor which constitutes the basic under-

pinning of the novel. The humor, of course, re-
sults not only from the notion of sexual regimenta-
tion, but also from the language used to describe
it in Pantoja's official reports. [5]

Pantoja's absurdist situations have had many anteced-
ents in the American screenplay, among them, Mister Rob-
erts, No Time for Sergeants, Stalag 17, Operation Mad Ball,
the comic scenes of The Caine Mutiny, and the television
series Sergeant Bilko. As mentioned above, Vargas Llosa
himself turned Pantoja into a screenplay that met the resistance of the Peruvian military: the armed forces were going
to begin recruitment of women and were afraid that "there
might be some unease among public sectors who might think
the women would end up as prostitutes. "[6]

Apparently, Vargas Llosa had originally written the
novel in three distinct versions. "In 1974, Vargas Llosa
spoke of first having written his work in his usual serious
style and then realizing that it was a failure," according to
William E. Siemens, "As he wrote it a second time, some
humor crept in, and the third and final writing resulted in
the thoroughly humorous text that was ultimately published."[7]
The last version evidenced our author's movement away from
structural complexity toward traditional storytelling. Both
the traditional nature of the screenplay and the last version
of the novel attest to Vargas Llosa's new spirit of composition. Vargas Llosa deliberately chose humor as a tool to
make the novel a parody of military organization in both
form and content. In an interview with one of his translators Vargas Llosa

"had believed--very foolishly of course--that
humor was dangerous to the type of literature I
wanted to write.... But the story I wanted to
write I discovered right away could be told only
with humor.... And so, I aimed at humor, and
it was a marvellous discovery; a whole world of
possibilities for literature opened up to me....
If it had been serious, the story of Pantaleón
Pantoja would have appeared as a straightforward
fable or as an anti-military parable. But as it's
narrated, I think it can be interpreted as something more complex. ... a parable about the
bureaucratic spirit itself. "[8]

Besides writing a condemnation of the military and

Peruvian "machismo," Vargas Llosa was also intensely interested in depicting the role of the intermediary in society,
"the person who carries out the commands and never ques-
tions why they are given. "[9]   The novel begins with a quote
from Gustave Flaubert's Sentimental Education: "There are
some men who serve as intermediaries among others; they
are treated like bridges and they advance further along. "
Besides borrowing this citation from Flaubert, Vargas Llosa
also uses his mentor's "third person technique and the device of making a place his central character: Flaubert's
Paris becomes Mr. Vargas Llosa's Peru. "[10]   But the multifaceted character of Pantoja is certainly attributable to Vargas Llosa's own Peruvian genius, which gives him a chance
to satirize many of the social clichés of contemporary Peru.
Because of Vargas Llosa's injection of humor into this latest
novel, many readers indeed felt that he was abandoning his
penchant for social criticism.   Vargas Llosa categorically
denies this assertion, believing that "humor allows a determined situation to be told at various levels of reality. "[11]
In fact, he has chosen to return to Peru, "in a whole world
of problems that constantly invade [him] and can come to be
asphyxiating. "[12]   Vargas Llosa never abdicates his role as
a social writer.   When he received the Rómulo Gallegos
Award in 1967 for The Green House, he stated his credo
for himself and his fellow writers, words worthy of repeti-
tion here:

> ... literature is fire, that it signifies non-conformism
> and rebellion, that the writer's very reason for
> being is protest, contradiction, criticism. ...   Lit-
> erature is a form of permanent insurrection and
> recognizes no strait-jackets.   Every attempt to
> change its angry, ungovernable nature will fail.
> Literature may perish but it will never conform. ...
> Our vocation has made us writers, the profession-
> al malcontents, the conscience of the unconscious
> disturbers of society, the rebels with a cause, the
> world's unredeemed insurrectionists, the intolerable
> devil's advocates.   I don't know if this is good or
> bad, I only know that it is so. [13]

Vargas Llosa provides some valuable guidelines for
his own work and for the future of the Latin American novel.
He believes that all his novels are

> realistic in their anecdotes, themes, characters,
> but they're not realistic in their structure. ...

> Almost none of my writing has a linear chronology,
> and the events are never distributed according to
> conventional space. In this sense there is a con-
> tradiction in my work, but only an apparent one.
> What interests me fundamentally is telling stories
> and in this sense, I think I'm a rather traditional
> writer. 14

Vargas Llosa is an astute evaluator of the current
Latin American literary scene. He notes that among his
fellow Latin American writers the evolution of a new kind of
literature, which he labels

> textual, literature that entirely scorns the prob-
> lems of plot, problems of character. It is a lit-
> erature of formal experimentalism, a type of writ-
> ing that interests me very little and bores me a
> great deal but has currently taken on importance
> in Latin America. 15

Clearly, Vargas Llosa strongly urges the return to traditional narrative forms, the art of "storytelling," as he has done
in Captain Pantoja and the Special Service. He also asks us
to reconsider some of the figures who are currently cele-
brating their fame and fortune in the blaze of the "boom,"
authors who write the "textual" literature, experimentalist
works, in which Vargas Llosa himself is no longer interested. A reading of Pantoja reveals the melodramatic
nature of Vargas Llosa's plots and his use of the most
familiar devices of pulp fiction but also his master craftsmanship, as well as his own use of some experimentalist
techniques, meticulously structured narratives, simultaneous
relation of several stories at once, "complexity," "montage"
effects, and fragmentation.

Although he admittedly has changed his mind about
the novels of Manuel Puig, Vargas Llosa's return to traditional storytelling might appear a retrogressive step in the
evolution of the Latin American novel. Surely his new pose
detracts readers and critics alike from some of the latest
works of Carpentier, Cortázar, García Márquez, Donoso,
Sarduy, Cabrera Infante, and even Puig, which although experimentalist in form have significant merits of their own.
As Mario Vargas Llosa's career is constantly shifting gears,
so are those of the other nine living writers considered in
this volume, each of whose oeuvre and its direction within
the realm of the "boom" of the Latin American novel is of

continual interest to readers and critics alike.   Vargas
Llosa's fascinating critique of Latin American literature
points the way for us to consider the next five writers
under scrutiny in this volume.

6. CABRERA INFANTE: CUBAN LYRICISM

When Guillermo Cabrera Infante's first novel, Three Trapped Tigers (or TTT, as it is often fondly referred to), appeared in the United States in 1971, translated from the "Cuban, " it caused an immediate sensation in literary circles. Among the reasons were its experimental form, its Latin American baroqueness, its collage effects, its insistence on a purely verbal reality compelling readers to reconstruct the language as they go because of the abundance of tongue-twisters, anagrams, palindromes, mystical images, linguistic puzzlers of all kinds cast adrift in an almost plotless sea of extraordinary language suggesting the chaotic totality of life. Vargas Llosa's prediction that "textual" literature would be the new cause of many Latin American writers certainly achieves a modicum of credence when we begin to examine closely the literary career of Cabrera Infante, which in itself is full of contrasts and contradictions.

Guillermo Cabrera Infante was born in 1929 in Gibara, Cuba, a small town on the northern coast of Oriente Province. He was the second child and first son of Guillermo Cabrera, a journalist and typographer, and his wife Zoila Infante, a local Communist. His early childhood was spent with his baby sister, going to kindergarten, reading comic strips, later attending a primary school (Los Amigos, run under Quaker auspices), and remembering the occasional arrests of his father and mother, who had founded the local Communist Party cell and were politically at loggerheads with the Batista regime. In 1941, at the age of twelve, Cabrera moved with his family to Havana, where his father worked for the newspaper Hoy. Throughout his studies for the bachillerato, begun at age fourteen, Cabrera became an avid reader, interested chiefly in the classics and American

magazines.   Dedicating himself to literature, at age eighteen
he wrote his first short story, a mediocre imitation of Angel
Asturias's El Señor Presidente, which was published, to his
surprise, by Bohemia, one of the leading Latin American
literary magazines of 1947.   Intending to follow a medical
career, Cabrera was forced to abandon this impossible
dream: he gave up his studies and began working as a
proofreader and secretary to the managing editor of Bohemia.
In 1949 he founded a literary magazine called Nueva Generación
and worked as a proofreader on several newspapers, among
them the Havana Herald, and as a ghost editor for Bohemia.

Returning to school in 1951, he entered Cuba's National School of Journalism.   Poverty forced him to work as
a translator, part-time pollster, and night watchman.   The
following year he graduated; founded a literary society,
Nuestro Tiempo, with a group of friends (which eventually
becomes a Communist-fronted organization); and created and
directed the Cinemateca al Cuba, an offspring of the
Cinémathêque Française.   Also in this year Cabrera met a
convent-school girl whom he married in 1953 at age twenty-
four.   In 1952 he began to write several short stories, one
of which, published in Bohemia, contained some English
four-letter profanities, for which he was jailed.   After his
release he had to use a pen name, "G. Cain," in order to
publish any stories or articles on cinema.   Under this
pseudonym he began to write a regular film column for
Carteles, Cuba's second-most-popular magazine.   His first
daughter was born in this year; shortly thereafter Cabrera
Infante left Cuba for the first time, visiting New York's
Museum of Modern Art to secure film prints for his Cinemateca.   Because he tried to use the Cinemateca as a political platform, the government dropped its support and closed
it down in 1956.

In the following year the Batista regime became even
more repressive, and Cabrera saw many of his friends
jailed by the Cuban police.   With Cuba rushing headlong to
the brink of the Castro revolution, Cabrera's literary activities became increasingly clandestine.   He briefly visited
Mexico and New York once again, was warned to cool down
the highly volatile political content of his columns (which
underwent strict censorship), and in 1958, the year his
second daughter was born, gathered many of the politically
slanted vignettes or short stories he wrote over the past
decade into the volume In Peace as in War, which finally
appeared in print in 1960 after going through several truncated editions.

With the outbreak of the Cuban revolution in 1959 and
Batista's abdication as dictator Cabrera Infante became editor of the newspaper Revolución, was appointed head of the
National Council for Culture, became an executive in the
newly created Cinema Institute, and founded and edited the
cultural weekly Lunes de Revolución. Favored by the Castro
regime at this time, he traveled with the Castro entourage
throughout the United States, Canada, and South America.
His travels increased in 1960, as he visited Europe, Russia,
East Germany, and Czechoslovakia with a delegation of
journalists; he in turn invited many writers to Cuba to get
to know the new revolutionary country.   Lunes de Revolución
moved on to Cuban television, and Cabrera Infante divorced
his first wife.

In 1961, because he organized a protest against the
censorship of the film P. M., which celebrated Havana night-
life of the 1960s and was made by his brother, the government banned Lunes de Revolución. Cabrera's protest was so
polemical, daring the government to deal with its first cultural controversy about the role of the artist and writer in
the revolution, that it led Fidel Castro to make his famous
speech "Words to the Intellectuals" and to the formation of
the Writer's Union.   Cabrera's organized protest, which had
the support of more than two hundred artists and writers,
caused the government to stage its first Congress of Cuban
Writers, putting the Lunes group into the untenable position
as being the only writers concerned with free expression left
in Cuba.   Sequestering of the film was officially condemned
and a jubilant Cabrera Infante was elected Vice-President of
a virtually ineffective Writer's Union.   At this low point in
his life, he married Miriam Gomez, a successful television,
film, and stage actress he had met in 1958, and began to
write She Sang Boleros, a continuation of his brother's film
P. M., about a black bolero singer, the microcosm of what
later became the novel Three Trapped Tigers (1964).

In 1962 Cabrera Infante became an internal exile.   He
published A Twentieth Century Vocation, a subversive book
of film reviews presented as a piece of fiction.   The book
sets out to prove that the only way a critic can survive under Communism is as a fictional character.   Banished from
Havana, he entered the diplomatic service and was sent to
Brussels as Cultural Attaché.   His short story collection In
Peace as in War was nominated for the International Prize
for Literature, becoming widely disseminated throughout
Europe.   Three Trapped Tigers, published in Spain under

the intentionally different title View of Dawn in the Tropics, won Spain's Biblioteca Breve Prize of 1964. (TTT was not published in its uncensored form in Spanish until 1967.) From 1962 to 1965 Cabrera Infante served with the Belgian Embassy, later becoming Chargé d'Affaires. On June 3, 1965, he returned to Cuba for his mother's funeral, a visit that led to his final disenchantment with the Cuban revolution. After narrowly missing the prestigious Formentor Prize, he severed all connections with the Cuban government on this last trip there, flying back to Europe with his daughters Ana and Carola.

Cabrera Infante has become one of the most celebrated Cuban exiles living in London. He lives there with his wife, children, and a Siamese cat named Diego Offenbach and earns a living writing short stories, film criticism, and screenplays.

During the early 1970s Cabrera Infante returned to the art of the essay, publishing O (1971), a book of random thoughts on diverse subjects in the pop mode. Exorcisms of Style (1976) is a collection of collages, pastiches, parodies, puns, and poetry, a personal Vanguardist look at life in the 1970s. He also wrote the screenplay for a Twentieth Century-Fox film, Vanishing Point, which failed badly at the box office. Arcadia Every Night (1978) is his most recent work, a series of five essays on North American cinema containing profiles of Howard Hawks, Orson Welles, and others. Also in the early 1970s he worked on the film script of Malcom Lowry's Under the Volcano, which was never produced, translated his own TTT (which appeared in English in 1971), and received a Guggenheim Fellowship to aid him in writing his second novel, View of Dawn in the Tropics, first published in Spain in 1974 (a new novel using an old title which masked the highly censored TTT) and appearing here in the United States in translation late in 1978.

Three Trapped Tigers may be Cabrera Infante's most formidable work to date, the novel that has accorded him his international reputation as one of Latin America's brightest literary superstars. TTT, according to David W. Foster, is

> a brilliantly loony memoir of life in Havana just before the Castro takeover ... an open novel ... a monumental game of literature or literature as a game. Cabrera Infante's position in the Latin

American novel seems assured by TTT, a novel
whose importance has been recognized by critics
and other novelists. 2

TTT represents the synthesis of the direction most
Latin American writers were taking at the peak of the literary "boom" of the mid-1960s.   It is the epitome of a plotless novel, completely experimental, a book that Vargas
Llosa would most undoubtedly detest.   It opens at Havana's
famous Tropicana nightclub, where an emcee presents several of the book's characters.   The novel is divided into
eight sections plus a prologue and an epilogue.   We are
cast adrift in Batista's tawdry Cuba of 1958, in a labyrinth
that has no real plot or protagonists, but consists of a
series of stories told with a Latin American baroqueness of
language.

The three trapped tigers of the title are Arsenio Cué,
an actor-writer, Codák, a photographer, and Silvestre, another writer.   Written in a collage-styled narrative prose
with cinematic montage effects, TTT describes the contact
(or lack of contact) these men make with the world that sur-
rounds them.   Arsenio Cué is apparently killed early on
when he confesses his love for the sensual Magdalena.   But
he was fired upon with blank bullets, and the protagonists
who really died are Estrella, the black singer "who always
sang boleros, " and Bustrófedon.   Cabrera describes a world
of prostitution and some bizarre sexual encounters inter-
mingled with the stories of a woman who goes to a psycho-
analyst, the "stories" of the Cuba Venegas nightclub, and
Bustrófedon's narrative--which form the principal plot.

Several secondary stories weave throughout the novel,
and there are parodies and cruel burlesques of fellow Cuban
writers, such as Alejo Carpentier, Lezama Lima, and Lydia
Cabrera.   The real problem in TTT is in knowing who is
narrating the events, since at once and the same time the
novel appears autobiographical and fictional.   One critic
summed up TTT's impact in this way:

A triple tongued sleeper of similies and tongue
twisters, Cabrera Infante combines chaotically
geography and genealogy, politics and perversion,
literature and lust, dreams and dialogue in a
parody of life which verges on caricature but
whose illusive mirrors of reality hide a profound
underlying sadness. 3

"TTT is an open-ended novel, " writes Foster, "which rejects customary structure and demands the reader reconstruct it as he reads and re-reads it. "[4] Many critics strike parallels between TTT and Cortázar's Hopscotch because of the same kind of externally imposed structure the true meaning of which is found within its interior rhythms and pattern of language.   Lack of structure may give the novel spontaneity, although it also leaves the reader with a sense of disorder.   Cabrera's novel, according to Souza, "explores the relationship between man's creative impulse and his desire to achieve immortality or permanence. "[5]   Foster writes:

> If Cortázar succeeds in reconciling the search for absolute values within the metaphysical chaos by a labyrinthian technique, Cabrera Infante proposes to bring to light the complexities behind the superficial appearances of present-day life in Cuba. [6]

Yet in both form and substance TTT was conceived in the mould of the anti-novel, with pretensions of aping Rabelais, Swift, Carroll, Faulkner, and even Joyce, pretensions that the author himself deems almost "unlimited" and still perceives as "unfulfilled. "

Cabrera Infante's latest novel, View of Dawn in the Tropics, is experimental, but is absolutely nothing like his first in style, form, rhythm, size, or characterization. View is a shorter work, only 141 pages, consisting mainly of a series of small ironic sketches tracing Cuban history from its earliest times to our own.   It contains none of the linguistic pyrotechnics (palindromes, anagrams, etc.), the black (or white) pages, diagrams, drawings, parodies, visual poems, and confusing narrative voices of its predecessor. View is a somber work, a serious experience, a sobering jolt after TTT.   It contains 103 sections narrated by a single voice (probably Cabrera Infante himself) on history, geography, war, death, and escape.   It represents a serious condemnation of Castro's regime.

The series of vignettes contain many cinematic devices.   The single unifying pose of the sometimes-elusive narrator is his insistence upon looking at old photographs and interpreting them for us.   His reminisences about the wars of 1868, 1898, and 1959 are conceived in cinematic freeze frames that describe a series of usually unidentified protagonists (with one single exception) with the rank of commandant, captain, doctor, or rebel.   The length, size, and cinematic style of the sketches are of varying quality, and there are only four literary liaisons or unifying elements between two or three of the 103 vignettes.

The longest entry is a mother's monologue described as a telephone call to the author about the death of her son Pedro Luis Boitel, who died for Cuba under the cruelties of the Castro regime.   Cabrera Infante's sketches are, according to the book's dust jacket, "contemporary--vivid and sharp, sometimes cruel and violent, sometimes witty, sometimes sad, frequently deeply ironical, ... a personal statement of the strategies of history. "[7]   View portrays presidents, generals, soldiers, blacks, Spaniards, Americans, rebels, and invaders and reveals the cruelties, hypocrisies, and tragedies that have washed over Cuban soil throughout the centuries.   It is Cabrera Infante's sardonic humor, combined with his irresistible, remarkable choice of detail, his ability to pinpoint events without identifying them, that makes his "experimental" View intriguing, bitterly amusing, and ultimately quite moving as he traverses the centuries of madness of human inhumanity.

One critic viewed the book as the author's attempt "to elevate to myth his central theme, Cuba ... to stop time and capture the elusive moment and endow it with a certain permanence, creating a new form, the ministory or micronarrative, or perhaps even a poem in prose, counterpointing two realities--the photographic with the real, and saw View as an exile's condemnation or vindication of his earlier pro-Castro series of short stories In Peace as in War. "[8]

As the book begins, we witness the creation of the island of Cuba at the dawn of time; we go through the exploration, exploitation, and evangelization phases of colonization, aware of the heavy impact of Spain and the dark side of the Spanish character, its injustices, brutalities, and cruelties against the Cuban people.   We pass through epochs of slavery (stylized similarly to the television documentary Roots), as rebellion against Spain bloodies the island.   Early on, Cabrera Infante is making an anti-war plea, demonstrating with continual heavy-handed irony how even the author of Cuba's National Anthem was put to death, how the poets and artists (much like us) died at the hands of a military that is also perceived as "accidentally" heroic.   There are bloodbaths of Haitian and Jamaican workers and gangster massa-

cres, Cuban-style.   On two occasions Cabrera describes
events that were the plots of major Hollywood films, John
Huston's We Were Strangers (digging through a cemetery to
assassinate a dictator) and Lewis Milestone's All Quiet on
the Western Front (describing the "lyrical" death of a rebel
by stray bullets from a comrade's rifle as he reaches up to
pick a mango).   Cabrera's cinematic sense never fails him.

Certain vignettes are elevated to allegorical proportions: a man being chased by "Tyranny," how "Death" took
the "Others."   We witness women losing their entire family,
wiping away their tears, and continuing to do their daily
wash.   Death indeed is a natural part of life in Cuba.   We
see soldiers machine-gunning mobs of people gathered in
front of a national palace by a dictator supposedly to witness
his abdication.   We view many treacheries and cruelties:
young boys single-handedly killing police lieutenants and then
handed over to the police by rebel leaders afraid of further
retribution; seven men machine-gunned one by one as they
leave their cover, giving themselves up to police; the coup
de grâce given men after being executed on Christmas Eve.
But Cabrera Infante lyrically elevates these last moments of
the victims; for example: "Before dying, did the last hostage
think he was dreaming?" (p. 70), or "He fell to one side and
rolled from the tree down toward the ravine.   What was he
thinking?   Someone once said that we never know what the
brave man thinks" (p. 99).

Cabrera Infante graphically describes the ugliness of
death, for example, in the comical episode of a homosexual
recaught by the police after he had tricked them previously,
"found a week later in the gutter.   They had cut off his
tongue and stuck it in his anus" (p. 78).   Or, "... the doctor took out a fistful of feces and among them, shining in
the sun, six, ten, twelve sharp little gray pieces of schrap-
nel: a splinter had hit him, splitting up in the intestinal
cavity as it entered, forming a shower of swift razors which
perforated his intestines and burst his liver" (p. 92).

Cabrera's intent was to write a serious anti-war
novel, with occasional seriocomic glimpses into the Cuban
character.   He documents, for example, attempted assassin-
ations that were successful on paper but disastrous in execu-
tion: ironically, "in the beauty of the gesture, destiny had
brought together heroism and failure" (p. 87).   He repeatedly demonstrates how the spontaneous act (of escape, for
example) is more successful than the well-planned plot.

View of Dawn in the Tropics is chock-full of
imagery--soldiers lying dead with holes in their necks,
bloody faces in a bucolic setting, ironically compared with
Renoir's Picnique sur l'Herbe; photographs that reveal "the
image of the dead hero when alive" (p. 119); lyrical images
of death: "... the volley or the single shot wasn't heard
but the impact is left and he will fall as long as man exists
and they will see him falling when eyes look at him and
they will not forget him as long as there is memory" (p.
115); "... his gray arm, next to the pale gray chest with
the black satin, falling on the black grass, leaning toward
the black earth and death forever..." (p. 115).

One incredible story, elevated to the level of parable,
demonstrates the dark side of the Cuban character.   A father, seeking to correct the nocturnal carousing habits of his
son asks his friend, the local Chief of Police, to arrest the
boy for a single night.   However, fate intervenes, and the
Police Chief is killed that evening by a bomb.   In retalia-
tion, the police choose ten political prisoners to be killed--
and the boy is among them.   Although entertaining as a
story, Cabrera Infante implies much more about the Cuban
mind, its penchant for practical jokes and cruelties, and
the tenuous role fate plays in life and death.   He also criti-
cizes the Cuban fetish for machismo, having some of his
fictional characters liken themselves to bullfighters.   The
revolution of 1959 was successful in one sense; it changed
the Cuban's attitude toward machismo.   Ballet dancer Jorge
Esquivel recently recalled the time when "people said they'd
rather see their sons clean streets than be a ballet dancer.
After the Revolution, Fidel went to see Alicia [Alonso], and
was so impressed by her that he decided to help her build a
ballet company in Cuba."9   In the main, however, View of
Dawn in the Tropics is an anti-Cuban, anti-Castro work.

In a somewhat autobiographical section, sprinkled with
imaginative details, Cabrera Infante recalls how they "took
my little theatre away from me" (p. 133); the perils of "na-
tionalization"; his own experiences cutting sugar cane; an in-
fection that led him to be sent home, eventually to flee the
country.   But his most biting critique of Cuba is his description of the death, after twelve years in prison, of Pedro
Luis Boitel, a student leader who "conspired against the
powers of the state."   Here Cabrera Infante takes pot shots
at the ineffectiveness of such international organizations as
the Red Cross, the OAS, the Commission on Human Rights,
as well as of Cubans themselves: "Not a single voice was

raised, nothing was said, nobody said a thing to get them to give him medical care ... not even the Pope ... because never has there been a Cuban, the God's honest truth, who has sacrificed himself for this country ..." (pp. 136-137).

    View of Dawn in the Tropics is an ironic book.   It describes what is really hidden under the exotic beauty of the Cuban landscape.   The dust cover carries the picture of a crocodile ready to bite.   View is a diatribe against war, against all sorts of tyrannies that are antithetical to the natural Cuban way of life.   Or is the real Cuban way of life so full of hypocrisy, guile, injustice, political schemes, see-saw skirmishes over the centuries always ending in petty dictatorships and eventual death?   People and plots are the real enemies, says Cabrera Infante.   The author depicts nature, not nostalgically but as an impersonal entity, immutable, unchanging, a mute spectator:

> And it will always be there.   As someone once said, that long, sad, unfortunate island will be there after the last Indian and after the last Spaniard and after the last African and after the last American and after the last Cubans, surviving all disasters, eternally washed over by the Gulf stream: beautiful and green, undying and eternal (p. 141).

Certainly, Mario Vargas Llosa would be pleased by Cabrera Infante's latest direction in his pursuit of perpetuating his narrative skill and his imaginative use of storytelling techniques.

7. FUENTES: MEXICAN ROOTS, MYTHS, IMAGES

Carlos Fuentes is the most widely known of the writers
mentioned in this book.   His novels, spanning a twenty-year
period, have all been successful here and abroad.   He is
the only one of these writers who has been able to make a
living solely from literature.   The only Mexican among
them, he is a controversial figure in his own country and
consequently has become an itinerant nomad, a self-imposed
exile, an émigré.   He is presently living in the United
States, dividing his time between lecturing and teaching at
both Columbia University and the University of Pennsylvania.

Born in Mexico City on November 11, 1928, the son
of a career diplomat, Carlos Fuentes was well educated at
the best schools in both North and South American capitals.
He learned English at the age of four in Washington, D. C. ,
and subsequently lived in Santiago, Rio de Janeiro, and
Buenos Aires before attending law school at the University
of Mexico.   He also spent some time at the Institut des
Hautes Etudes Internationales in Geneva and from 1950 to
1952 was a member of the Mexican delegation to the International Labor Organization, also in Geneva.

In 1952 Fuentes became a Marxist and joined the
Communist Party, breaking with his family and Mexico's
middle classes.   The following year he gave up his career
as a student of international law and diplomacy in order to
be independent as a writer.   His break with the diplomatic
corps was short-lived: he finished his law degree and in
1954 returned from Geneva, after taking advanced studies
in International Relations, to become assistant head of the
press section of the Ministry of Affairs, serving in a similar capacity at the University of Mexico between 1955 and

1956 and as head of the Department of Cultural Relations at Mexico's Ministry of Foreign Affairs between 1957 and 1959.

During these years, 1954 to 1958, Fuentes surfaced as a writer.   In 1955 he became co-founder with Emmanual Carballo of the Revista mexicana de literatura and later edited and co-edited El Espectador, Siempre, and Política. Since 1959 he has devoted himself exclusively to writing-- novels, short stories, book reviews, political essays, travel pieces for Holiday, literary criticism, film scripts (for Luis Buñuel and other directors), and plays.

Fuentes is well known for the enormous discipline he exercises as a writer, spending five to six hours at his desk every day, which has produced a steady stream of fiction and other pieces since 1958.

Fuentes, like Vargas Llosa, is politically active and has been outspoken on many major political and intellectual issues.   He has been considered an independent public figure of Mexico's and Latin America's left.   His stance against the U. S. intervention in the Dominican Republic, his support of Castro's Cuban revolution, and his opposition to this country's Alliance for Progress Program has made him, at times, persona non grata in the United States.   In 1969, the year of his divorce, Fuentes was denied entry into Puerto Rico, which led to many liberal attacks on the United States' immigration policy.   Fuentes was also excluded from Mexico because of his own country's brutal repression of students at the Olympic Games "massacre" of 1968.   Becoming an exile, he spent several years in Paris, but returned to Mexico in 1971, acting as a spokesperson for "leftist" intellectuals and labor leaders who created a new informal political organiza- tion to challenge, by nonviolent methods, the one-man/one- party rule of the dominant Institutional Revolutionary Party. He served as Mexico's ambassador to France before settling in the United States in 1978.

On the other side of the coin, Fuentes's political commitment has coincided with contemporary liberal attitudes. He was critical of the Soviet Union's bad treatment of writers like Solzhenitsyn; he spoke of the thaw in the cultural cold war on the part of the United States, which caused him con- siderable criticism in Havana in 1966.   But Fuentes's main interest has always been Mexico--the essence of Mexican reality, its roots, its myths--even though he may have spent several years abroad.   As exile, émigré, or nomad,

Fuentes's major preoccupations are with the failure of the Mexican revolution of 1910, the national preoccupation with Mexican identity, and the role of the past in Mexico's contemporary society. His stance has earned him the hostility of the Mexican "establishment" but the fervent admiration of a new generation of free-thinkers, who look to him for ideological leadership. [1]

Ebullient, excitable, and extremely creative, Carlos Fuentes writes continuously, and each work is entirely different from the previous ones. Regarding influences on his writing, Fuentes pulls the critic's leg, saying that Zane Grey is the only author who ever made an impact on his career. Of course, if we look further, we can see that William Faulkner, John Dos Passos, Octavio Paz, and certain introspective poets, such as José Gorostiza, have deeply influenced this extremely innovative and dynamic writer.

His first book was Masked Days (1954), a collection of six surrealistic short stories about the presence of the myths and mysteries of ancient Mexico in contemporary life. Fuentes received a fellowship in 1956 from the Centro Mexicano de Escritores that gave him the leisure to write his first novel. Where the Air Is Clear (1958) won him immediate international recognition and was subsequently published in twelve languages. Written in an experimental style reminiscent of Galdós, Dos Passos, and Faulkner, the book was an extraordinary biography of a city, a synthesis of present-day Mexico. Vargas Llosa called it "a mural painting, pullulating and populous, "[2] full of acrid insights, cinematic techniques, a wide spectrum of characters, a masterwork, a panorama of Mexico City life from the revolution of 1910 to 1958. (As a student at the University of Mexico in 1959, this author noted the impact of Fuentes's first novel on his fellow college students, Americans and Mexicans alike, who found its new style too complex, too cynical, too difficult to comprehend. The book provoked widespread literary debates and discussions throughout the university.)

In 1959 Fuentes published The Good Conscience, a rather unsuccessful realistic novel, semiautobiographical and written in the manner of Galdós. The book was about the adolescence of a young provincial rebelling against his middle-class family but finally being absorbed into the comforts of his class. Conscience strengthened Fuentes's career and writing techniques, but it was The Death of Artemio Cruz (1962), exploring the consciousness of a dying patriot, that

solidified his international reputation.   Fuentes borrowed
cinematic techniques from Orson Welles's Citizen Kane and
literary ones from the nouveau roman movement, revealing
the facets of Artemio's biography while utilizing three narrative voices and erratic time shifts, all of which make the
novel a difficult, complex work.   Its main themes--the revolutionary idealism of a robber caudillo presented in contrast
to his loveless marriage, brief love affair, and the cynical
ruthlessness that characterized his rise to power--are extraordinarily hard to follow.   But like his earlier novels,
Fuentes orchestrated a rich tour de force, depicting once
again the failure of the revolution of 1910, as Artemio Cruz
recalls scenes in his life from the horrors of the revolution
to the present.

     Using the technique of the second-person narrative
(as he had in Artemio Cruz), Fuentes in 1963 wrote the
novella Aura, a kind of reworking of Henry James's The
Aspern Papers, in which he tried to recapture the historical
past symbolically in his pursuit of the Jamesian fantasy-
reality theme.   Aura was a relatively slight work, a literary
exercise that met with little success.   Quickly thereafter
Fuentes published his second series of short stories, Tales
of the Blind (1964), which continued his explorations into
such themes as the corruption of innocence, the monstrosi-
ties that lurk behind the events of everyday life, and the
confusions of personal identity.   It did little to advance his
career but was a showcase for a particularly popular story,
"The Doll Queen, " which has since appeared in numerous
Latin American short-story collections.

     In 1967 Fuentes published Holy Place, an undistin-
guished novella dealing with the relationship between a Mexican movie star and her psychologically unstable son, told
through the use of Greek myths.   In March of 1967 the
manuscript of A Change of Skin, his sixth novel (and eighth
book), won the coveted Biblioteca Breve Prize in Spain for
best novel that year.   Unpublished because of Spanish censorship, it finally appeared in Mexico in 1968 and in English at
the same time.   In it, Fuentes successfully fused his "experimental style" with the fantasy-reality theme that has always fascinated him.   The book depicts one day in the life
of four people (a Mexican professor, his Jewish-American
wife, his mistress Isabel, and his wife's European Nazi
lover) forced to spend the night in a motel in Cholula, probing, through the use of flashbacks, the vapidity of their lives
and the general decadence of European and American bourgeois society.   Monegal writes:

Fuentes mixed the Aztec myths with the pop,
modish present and moved the action back and forth
from Mexico to Czechoslovakia, from sacrificial
rites in a pyramid to the technological horrors of
a Nazi concentration camp as narrated mostly by
Freddie Lambert, a cab driver.[3]

Although the mixture of locales was not always successful,
critics felt that some of the episodes were among the best
Fuentes had ever written, seeing the book's fundamental concern as the primitive but indestructible notions of vengeance
and atonement. Some critics thought the novel overburdened
with symbolism, fashionable stylistic devices, and capricious
narrative techniques, but saw it as a work "close to great-
ness. " In Spain the novel was viewed as pornographic, com-
munistic, and anti-Christian.

At about the same time Fuentes turned to the essay
to express his rage at Mexican authorities for the firing upon
students at an Olympic Game rally in 1968; it was published
as Paris: The May Revolution. A shorter, allegorical
novel, Birthday (1969), again dealt with the fantasy-reality,
space-time themes, and was reminiscent of the short stories
of Jorge Luis Borges. A book of essays, The New Spanish
American Narrative, also appeared at the end of 1969. It
discussed the careers and literature of Vargas Llosa, García
Márquez, Cortázar, and several others, including the
Spaniard Juan Goytisolo.

Fuentes, at this period, may have run "thematically
dry" and took a break from writing novels to engage his
mind in essays, screen treatments, and plays. He worked
with Academy Award-winner Abby Mann (Judgement at Nurem-
berg) on a screen adaptation of Oscar Lewis's brilliant socio-
logical tract The Children of Sánchez; with Luis Buñuel on a
film adaptation of Alejo Carpentier's novella The Hunt; and
with García Márquez on an original screenplay, a western
entitled Time to Die. Fuentes wrote two plays: All Cats
Are Gray and The One-Eyed Man Is King, both published
and presented in 1970. Three collections of essays appear--
House with Two Doors (1970), The Mexican Scene (1971),
and Bodies and Offerings (1973)--before his magnum opus
Terra Nostra is published in 1975. Begun in London in
1968 and completed in Virginia in 1974, Terra Nostra is
Fuentes's most ambitious novel to date.

It would take an entire chapter to deal with the design

and plot of Terra Nostra, a gigantic novel that novelist and
critic Juan Goytisolo in a brilliant twenty-page article has
called "the supreme example of a total literary creation....
Terra Nostra is not only Carlos Fuentes' major work. It
is also beyond any doubt one of the greatest monuments of
the Spanish language novel. "4 Through myth, fiction, and
chronicle, writes Goytisolo, Fuentes's monumental novel depicts the discovery and conquest of the New World, starting
with the roots of that epic struggle in Europe. Terra Nostra
represents the culmination of all of Fuentes's literary expertise and experiments, a colossal 350, 000-word opus, a kind
of panoramic Hispano-American creation myth, spanning
twenty centuries and embracing virtually the whole European
and American (especially Mexican) culture and civilization.
Fuentes set out to do what García Márquez accomplished in
The Autumn of the Patriarch, to create a narrative that is
told simultaneously by several characters, producing a collective voice.

Philip II, Terra Nostra's chief protagonist, is used
to present the novel's central enigma--how a people whose
power is based upon the absence of life created and lost an
entire civilization through the accumulation of its own
expansionist-claustrophobic contradictions. It is Fuentes's
retelling of this history, an accumulation of these contradictions, that is, according to Goytisolo, the raw thematic material and stylistic basis for Terra Nostra.

American critics have not been too receptive to
Fuentes's longest novel, calling it excessive, surreal,
baroque, a masterpiece, unreadable, exhausting, humorless,
magical, unique, greatly perceptive, compelling, audacious,
breathtaking, inventive (with its animated paintings, talking
mirrors, time machines and metamorphosing mummies), a
magnificent failure. 5

Fuentes continues to surprise us with his versatility.
When in France in the summer of 1977, he completed a
manuscript entitled The Hydra Head (published here in 1978),
a controversial world-class thriller, a spy novel fulfilling
his dual task as a writer: "... to participate as an intellectual in the struggle for basic change in Latin America,
and as an artist to remain responsible to his art by what-
ever techniques and approaches to reality which will serve
his creative aims. "6

The Hydra Head takes its title from the mythological

monster referred to in Pierre de Corneille's play Cinna,
but is updated as a Third World menace: "Like the Hydra,
the oil is reborn, multiplied from a single severed head"
(p. 292). Fuentes continues in the last lines of the novel:
"Dark semen in a land of hopes and betrayals, oil fecundates
the realms of the Malinche beneath the mute voices of stars
and their nocturnal portents" (p. 292). Fuentes's use of the
hydra-head symbol and his intention to awaken the Mexican
national conscience to its participation in international petro-
politics elevates The Hydra Head from an ordinary but intriguing Third World espionage novel to a thesis novel. The
implications of The Hydra Head go far beyond its plot, which
is straight out of a 1940s Hollywood scenario. Fuentes is
intentionally aping the classic 1943 film Casablanca, dedicating this novel to the memory of Peter Lorre, Sydney
Greenstreet, Conrad Veidt, and Claude Rains "in strict order of disappearance." Fuentes's problem is that he mixes
up equal parts of Casablanca with the screenplays of two
other Humphrey Bogart films, notably The Maltese Falcon
and Dark Passage, all to our cinematic amazement, coming
away with a somewhat jumbled and absurd plot.

The Hydra Head is divided into four parts organized
into forty-nine chapters with an epilogue. In Part One, "His
Own Host," we are introduced to nearly all the protagonists.
Felix Maldonado ("happy evil-doer") is Fuentes's first real
hero, a James Bond of underdevelopment, a lawyer-
economist who works as the Chief of the Bureau of Cost
Analysis for the federal government in Mexico City. In a
straightforward chronological style Fuentes unwinds his tale
of Felix's attendance at a presidential award ceremony, his
"blackout," his supposed attempt to assassinate the President, his own murder, his waking up into a new identity as
"Diego Velásquez," and his attempts to recapture his former
life as Felix with his wife Ruth, his mistress Mary Rosen-
berg, and his idealized love Sara Klein, just returned from
Israel. As in Julio Cortázar's A Manual for Manuel, Felix's
blackout represents his "black spot," the unconscious experience that provides illumination for him at the end of the
novel--why he lost consciousness, who was buried in his
place, who murdered Sara Klein, and how he will assume
his new identity in a world of CIA agents, Mexican spies,
and Arab oil interests against a background of danger and
intrigue.

Part Two, "The Mexican Agent," presents Felix waking up in a sleazy hospital on Calle Tonaloa under the care

of Licha, a nurse who helps him recover from plastic surgery. He discovers his obituary in the newspapers as
"Felix Maldonado" and also the murder of Sara Klein. After
recuperating and escaping from a hospital fire (designed to
provide cover for his flight to freedom from an insidious
Director General on the President's staff) Felix/Diego comes
across a phonograph record of Sara's voice that recounts her
entire biography and her love for Jamil, a Palestinian; her
affair with Bernstein, Felix's former economics professor;
and her idealized love for our protagonist. Fuentes tries
to confuse us, switching to a new narrator in the first-
person singular and then suddenly reverts to the third-person
voice of Felix. (In Part Four Fuentes reveals, as in all
good thrillers, the identity of the "I," Felix's former Mexican roommate at Columbia University and the head of a
Mexican petroleum combine, whose sister Angelica Rossetti
is murdered in a plot designed to force Felix to reveal the
whereabouts of a mysterious diamond ring--a ring that
Angelica had stolen from Bernstein and that Felix gave to a
mysterious Captain Harding for safe transport on his ship
departing from Galveston and bound to Coatzacoalcos. --
Sounds a bit like The Maltese Falcon.)

Part Three, "Operation Guadalupe," deals with a plot
by Israeli agents to secure the exact geographical locations
of Mexican oil fields in order to ensure the stability of their
own country in the constantly shifting relationship between
the United States and Arab petroleum interests. Lasers used
to photograph Mexican oil refineries, holograms affixed to the
facets of the mysterious diamond ring, and Felix's attempt to
solve the murder of Sara Klein are dealt with in this section
as Felix begins to assume his new identity.

The final section of the novel, "War With the Hydra,"
introduces us to the narrator, "Timon of Athens," as master
spy who played the roles of Trevor, a Houston agent, and
Mann, a New York spy, among others. "Timon" reveals to
Felix the point of Felix's "murder"--first to assassinate the
President and then to blame Israel for it, shifting Mexico
into a prime position for OPEC participation. As in thriller's, the entire "black spot" of Felix's own assassination is
revealed, how he was drugged with propanol, how Jamil was
substituted, jailed, and later killed in place of Felix, how
the holograms in the ring were made and used as bait for
Arab and Israeli agents. Felix also learns that Sara's death
was the result of Mary's cuckolded husband Abie's jealousy
and that his own wife Ruth (dressed in a nun's habit to

provide a distraction for a mariachi group) pushed Abie into committing the crime, cutting Sara's throat in a sleazy hotel room.   But Ruth's jealousy was not the only element in the plot to kill Sara.   There are national villains: "The Hydra of our passions is trapped in the talons of the bicephalous eagle" (p. 283).   As Felix is about to resume his relationship with his wife, we wander as Diego did, into another presidential reception at the National Palace and wonder if history will repeat itself, if another assassination attempt will take place.   Only the novel's two-page epilogue helps us to transcend the previous 290 melodramatic pages that came before it.

The Hydra Head is Carlos Fuentes's newest literary creation and a timely one in light of Mexico's newly discovered reserves of oil.   It is also entertaining, concise, and fast-moving, like a James Bond film full of chases, suspense, and shoot-outs.   On one level, it is pure melodrama.   We want Felix to solve all the mysteries.   Subsequently, we try to fit the characters to their Casablanca cinematic equivalents: Sinon Ayub plays the Peter Lorre role, Bernstein is Greenstreet, Trevor is Veidt and also Claude Rains, as he admits in an exchange with Felix.   Felix's Rick or Bogart hero is always seen in counterpoint to Sara Klein's Ilsa: their theme song is "Mack the Knife" instead of "As Time Goes By. "

Apart from these campy, cinematic considerations, Fuentes includes some literary allusions, in the spy jargon, to Alice in Wonderland and to Hamlet.   The characters are all extremely well developed in this straight storytelling approach--one that Vargas Llosa would applaud.   The novel is also excellent in portraying the ambiences of Mexico City's diverse sections, the Zona Rosa and Coyacán, as well as Houston, Galveston, and the port city of Coatzacoalcos.   Fuentes's pro-Jewish sympathies are apparent in this fictional work, as are his fears of American aggression for Mexican oil.   In sum, Hydra Head is a novel chock-full of action, sexuality, and style and mixes the reality-fantasy theme, one of Fuentes's perennial favorites.

> "For you, it began in a taxi, remember?   That was the moment of your return, Felix, that unknowing step from reality to nightmare, the moment when everything that seems real and secure in your life slips away and becomes uncertain, unsure and phantasmagoric" (p. 241).

It is full of machismo, sensuality, and much good writing.
Fuentes portrays Mexico as a corrupt, fragmented society,
out of contact and, at times, under no governmental con-
trols whatsoever (regarding, specifically, Mexico's press).
He implies that these conditions are prevalent today and that
there is resistance to the kind of oppression we witness in
the novel. The Hydra Head offers no solutions to the present government's dilemma about the newly discovered oil
fields. Fuentes seems to stand apart from his creation, a
cynical observer, suggesting on the novel's last page that
history repeats itself for Felix as it does for the nation.

What Carlos Fuentes has given us with The Hydra
Head is a concise portrait of Mexico and Mexicans, a con-
siderable change of pace after the overwhelming size and
scope of Terra Nostra. However, he has provided us with
merely an entertainment, not a tour de force, a gutsy novel
written with fun, verve, Kafka-esque plots, preposterous
coincidences, and betrayals. The cinematic images and
codes amuse us at times; but Hydra Head is more a spoof
of the classic spy thriller, than a political commentary.
One critic felt that the novel was "politically crude"[7] and
pamphleteering to the point of showing up the Israeli's as
bad guys, even though Mexico would be better off staying
out of OPEC. Anthony Burgess writes:

> Carlos Fuentes half lulls us into the expectation
> of a mere thriller, and the movie-buffery of the
> hero, Felix Maldonado, confirms that we ought
> not to expect much more than blood, the chase,
> the pedantic loquacity of Greenstreet villains.
> ... perhaps the true distinction [of the novel] re-
> sides in its having dispensed with the possibilities
> of the spy thriller as a serious form. [8]

It will be interesting to see the future direction of
Carlos Fuentes's fiction. He is a writer of unquestionable
talent, ability, and promise. Although Hydra Head does not
augur well in terms of his creative development, it nevertheless represents a new polarity for him, a divergence
from "experimentalist" techniques and a return to the traditional narrative--but one always rooted in images and myths
perennially linked to his private cosmos: Mexico and its
goals for mejicanidad, or a common lifestyle shared by all.

8. PUIG: ARGENTINE "CAMP"

The chief influence on the writing of Manuel Puig has been
the motion picture. In previous chapters we have seen how
Carlos Fuentes's The Hydra Head was written much like a
screenplay, how Cabrera Infante's experiences as a film reviewer and director of a cinémathêque helped him to reveal
more deeply the realities of action and character in his
novel Three Trapped Tigers, and how Vargas Llosa's return to straight storytelling techniques helped him to turn
his novel Captain Pantoja and the Special Service into a
film. The influence of motion pictures, however, was in-
cidental to the careers of these novelists. Only Manuel Puig
could be considered an experimentalist whose language of
reality is the language of the cinema, but always in the context of Argentina and her people. Film and the media are
the energizing forces and creative outlets in all of Puig's
fiction. Like most of the writers in this volume, Manuel
Puig also considers himself an exiled Argentinian, one who
returns periodically to his native country. "Although I was
blacklisted there, I need the context of Argentina. I am
not a universal writer. "[1]

   Manuel Puig was born in the small town of General
Villegas in the Argentine pampas in December of 1932. His
mother worked as a chemist at the local country hospital;
his father was a local businessman. At the age of four Puig
began his daily film-going. He considered himself the "best"
student up to the age of ten, when, in 1942, his addiction
for movies really set in, overtaking his academic interests.
Because his favorite films were such Hollywood dramas as
Gone With the Wind and Rebecca, he was inspired to learn
English and became number one in his class. When he was
eleven, he reports, a baby brother of his died and "a fifteen

80

year old boy tried to rape me ... [and] I stopped growing
physically for three years. "2

When Puig reached adolescence in 1946 he began
secondary school as a boarder in Buenos Aires (about twelve
hours away by train from Villegas), there being no schooling
beyond the elementary in that small pampas town.   Puig reportedly missed his mother terribly, found his schoolmates
cruel, and escaped reality on weekends at matinees of a
first-run Buenos Aires movie house, where he saw such
films as Mildred Pierce and Saratoga Trunk.   Salvador
Dali's cinematic conception of Freud as recreated in Hitch-
cock's film Spellbound had such a profound effect upon the
adolescent Puig that he began a program of reading apart
from his routine lessons.   He took up volumes by Gide,
Hesse, and Sartre and expanded his cinema horizons to include foreign films other than American imports.   After seeing Henri Clouzot's Jenny L'Amour in 1947 he decided he
wanted to be a film director; as a consequence, he began to
study French, English, and Italian--the languages of the
cinema.

By 1950 Manuel Puig was eighteen and still smitten
with Hollywood heroines like Ingrid Bergman, Joan Craw-
ford, and Rita Hayworth.   He finished secondary school that
year and entered the School of Architecture at the University
of Buenos Aires.   After an unsuccessful trial year he
switched to the School of Philosophy; he kept up with his
study of languages but was always drawn to film work.   He
bought copies of Photoplay surreptitiously and became interested in the careers of several Hollywood directors, especially George Stevens and Billy Wilder, whose abilities were
at their zenith with such important films as A Place in the
Sun and Sunset Boulevard.   In 1953 Puig spent one awful
year in military service and served as a translator for the
Air Force.   By the time he completed his language studies
at a private institute, he was fluent in French, English, and
Italian.   In 1955 he received a small scholarship to travel
to Rome, where he tried, in 1956, to break into Cinecittà
Studios.   With no connections, Puig spent two futile years--
one in Rome, the other in Paris--failing to find his niche in
European filmmaking.

When he was twenty-eight he arrived in London, an
Argentine immigrant, washing dishes at a theater restaurant
and giving lessons in Spanish and Italian to earn a living.
It was at this time he wrote his first film script, which he

describes as a sort of Wuthering Heights, intended for
Vivien Leigh.   "What excited me in film was to copy, not
to create."[3] In 1959 he wrote another unsuccessful, unpro-
duced film script in Stockholm entitled Summer Indoors.
Both scripts suffered from broken English, although the latter tried to reproduce the witty dialogue inspired by those
Cary Grant-Irene Dunne films like My Favorite Wife or
Pennies from Heaven.   Puig desperately wanted to write in
good English, in the dialogued style of the 1930s and 1940s,
but was finally told by his friends to begin writing in Spanish.

Returning to Argentina in 1960, for a short time he
worked as an assistant director in the Argentine film indus-
try, which at that time produced about thirty films annually
under the Peronista regime.   He left Argentine films because he could not stand to work under pressure or any type
of aggression as a scenarist.[4] It was at this time he wrote
his first film script in Spanish, "not the Castilian language
of bad films but the Argentine language of reality."[5] Returning to Rome in 1961, he spent some time at the Institute
of Cinematography, working fleetingly with an Italian film
crew (which he disliked) for a short time.   He also began
to write some sketches of his life in Villegas in the 1940s
in Spanish, sketches also about his cousin, his romances,
his relatives.   Before leaving Rome, Puig knew he had begun a novel.   In 1963 he moved to New York City, while
continuing work on his first novel.   He took a not-too-
demanding job for three years with Air France at Kennedy
Airport.   One day, while working at Air France's Manhattan
office, he reportedly sold an air ticket to Greta Garbo, one
of his favorite movie queens.

Puig speaks of these years in New York, from 1963
to 1965, as the happiest he had ever had since his childhood
days of 1940-43.   He finished the manuscript of his first
novel and took a vacation in Tahiti (via an Air France em-
ployee ticket).   His experience in writing film scripts certainly helped him to create his first novel, Betrayed by Rita
Hayworth.   Finished in manuscript in December of 1965,
Betrayed was a finalist for the Best Novel Award offered by
Seix Barral Publishers of Barcelona.   It was not until 1968,
however, that Betrayed was published in Buenos Aires, after
three years of contested contracts and censorship problems.
Although the literary critics were cool to Betrayed when it
finally appeared, Puig had hit upon his future vocation: "I
had been working freely, without thinking of pleasing any-
body, just trying to express myself on my own terms."[6]

Sometime before Betrayed by Rita Hayworth appeared, Puig began his second novel, which was to be published as an old-fashioned serial in a magazine.   But after seeing the first few chapters, the magazine decided to reject it.   However, when Betrayed was selected by Le Monde, Paris's leading literary journal, as one of the best novels of 1968-69, the serial, entitled Heartbreak Tango, was published in Buenos Aires.   It became an instant best-seller.   Betrayed was then republished, and it was accorded the acclaim it deserved the previous year.   Although Betrayed by Rita Hayworth was called "a masterpiece, full of literary allure ... [with] plenty of plain panache and strut ... [and] a dazzling and wholly original debut"[7] for Puig, it was Heartbreak Tango that, for the first time in Puig's writing career, turned a profit.   This gave the author confidence to begin a new novel, a thriller tentatively titled The Buenos Aires Affair, which was published in that city in 1973.

In an interview at New York's New School of Social Research in 1976, Manuel Puig had some important information to reveal about his life, especially his career as a writer.   When he first began to write Betrayed by Rita Hayworth, Puig admitted it was the voices of the characters themselves that influenced him.   He did not like to write in the third person but allowed each character to tell his or her own story through diaries, letters, and monologues.   In Betrayed Puig wrote about people he knew well and who let him share their intimate moments.   Puig characterizes his characters as a "gallery of misfits, people from the town of Villegas who have lots of time on their hands, defeated people, in bad 'psychological' shape. "[8]   Betrayed "explores the world of the rootless sons of middle-class immigrants, whose 'traditions, ' sardonically viewed against the implicit gaucho background of Argentine literature, consist of women's magazines, Hollywood films, radio and TV soap operas, and the banal lyrics of tangos and boleros. "[9]   It was the sensitive story of a treacherous boy named Toto, who was obsessed with the romantic dreams generated by Hollywood movies. For him and other characters in the novel, writes Latin American critic Monegal,

> Hollywood is more real than the desolate, ugly town in the pampas they are condemned to, and Rita Hayworth's betrayal of Tyrone Power in Rouben Mamoulian's [technicolor] version of Blood and Sand is more moving than the betrayals they commit in their everyday existence.   Movies for them are not

only a source of verbal or artistic experience--
they are the only real life. [10]

It was Puig's vision not only to record nostalgically his mental return to his early Argentine life but "to expose the roots
of that alienated society ... re-creating in minute detail the
horrid existence of men and women whose only contact with
beauty and romance was in their excursions to the cinema."[11]
Monegal believes Puig is one of the generation that utilized
film as analysis, "the generation which learned to dream and
write in darkened theaters, adapted the social and erotic patterns offered by the commercial North American film and
was educated, not colonized, by celluloid."[12]

This formative aspect of film on Puig's aesthetic life
and education is manifested in the "alienation" of his characters and in his transposition of an alienated spoken language to written language, using the techniques of pop art to
communiate a complex vision of his own world.   It is this
cinematic influence that makes Betrayed by Rita Hayworth
and Puig's subsequent novels some of the most original contemporary Latin American narratives.   Betrayed's chief
character, Toto, may also be Puig's most autobiographical
creation; the novel may have been the author's attempt to
reveal the "miseducation" that limited his growth as a real
human being. [13]

Although Puig admitted himself that the material he
used in Betrayed by Rita Hayworth "wasn't too good"[14] and
that one could never really get inside the characters of the
novel, his second attempt at fiction, Heartbreak Tango, deserves the critical acclaim it was accorded (and the sale of
one hundred thousand copies in Argentina alone).   It is a
very cinematic treatment of a woman, Nené, who speaks in
an idealized romantic pattern derived from an overexposure
to Hollywood films, a working-class woman whose love for a
treacherous Don Juan-type is a figment of her cinematic inspiration.   Puig, according to Rodríguez Monegal, uses
"melodrama and the style of cheap novelettes to reveal the
frustrated dreams of a whole country ... whose only real
education consisted of the soap operas and tango lyrics heard
over the radio."[15]

In relating the chronicle of Juan Carlos, and the
women who loved him so desperately, in installments, Puig
reveals progressively the characters of the women, telling
their story through their own words, employing cheap,

sentimental lyrics from well-known tangos and boleros to describe their intimate feelings. He also uses the cinematic techniques of montage and cross-cutting between pathetic and crudely realistic scenes, "from the heights of frustrated love to the mechanics of fornication, ... shaping characters both from the inside of their dream and from the outside of their predictable actions."[16] Romantic movies are the model of conduct for Puig's characters under all circumstances. Puig admittedly "kept his own narrative voice out of the action of the novel, [assuming] the reality of their world is what culture imposes upon them."[17] Puig himself felt he had utilized his own cinematic and serialized techniques appropriately to create a "simultaneity of action for his characters."[18] He would have preferred to have called the novel Orchids in the Moonlight and capitalize on his combination of pastiche and parody of the romantic trash he created in order to transcend "camp," rather than contribute to it.[19] Many critics thought Heartbreak Tango to be "a moving novel, a comic, complex work, brilliant and forceful, a melancholic arabesque of a novel" and Puig, "a brilliant writer, a funny writer or a tenderly elegiac one."[20]

In The Buenos Aires Affair, published in 1973, Puig presents in the form of a detective story with anticlimaxes the story of sculptor Gladys Hebe D'Onforio and her lover Leo Druscovich, an art critic, and how their success is thwarted by their respective masturbatory obsessions and their sado-masochistic affair. Puig blames the contemporary movie ethos that "sex is the true key to happiness" for the destruction of real compassion and love between the protagonists. He recycles the detective-story formula of an old forties film--The Maltese Falcon (1941) or This Gun for Hire (1942), for example--to reveal the hidden realities of Argentina. Puig dazzles us with an impressive use of stylistic techniques--stream of consciousness, parody, Hollywood epigraphs--and a clever use of lists and footnotes that goes far beyond the traditional scope of a simple detective story. His special fondness for the footnote surfaces once again in his most recently translated novel, Kiss of the Spiderwoman (1979). However, Emir Rodríguez Monegal feels Buenos Aires Affair is very successful, another sustained bravura performance, "in which exploding his character's dreams, exposing them for what they are--mere fakes, pallid substitutes for the authentic personal experience and feeling denied them by the social alienation from which they suffer."[21] Monegal sees Puig as "a moralist and consummate master in portraying subtleties and depths

of social reality"[22] and his novel, the stuff his character's
dreams are made of. The book has been characterized as
"an intensely moving novel about love and victimization."[23]

A dark-haired, brown-eyed, sensitive man, Manuel
Puig remains a bachelor, self-exiled in New York. When
this author last saw him in 1976, he had just begun Kiss of
the Spiderwoman, and mentioned that The Buenos Aires Affair had been banned in Argentina.

As this book was going to press Puig's latest novel,
Pubis angélical (Angel Hair; 1979), appeared in Barcelona.
The book tells two parallel stories. The first is set in the
1930s in Albuquerque, New Mexico, and is related in cinematic terms; the second is about a contemporary infirm
Argentine woman who narrates her past love affairs while
commenting on life under Argentina's present dictatorial
military regime. Both stories show women who are used
by their men; both are about unfortunate love affairs. The
first is told in a suspenseful science-fiction scenario; the
second is in a completely developed realistic mode, showing
Puig's excellent ear for conversation and the "rightness" of
language and keen observations into feminine psychology.

Kiss of the Spiderwoman is Puig's best translated
novel to date, a thoughtful, controlled performance. Although he uses a number of familiar stylistic devices--
"hyped-up Hollywood style movie plots, clinical psychological analyses of sexuality and stream-of-consciousness dialogue,"[24] Spiderwoman capitalizes upon camp and also presents its readers with a moving homosexual love affair between two prisoners in a Buenos Aires jail circa 1978.

Molina, a thirty-eight-year-old window dresser and a
confessed corruptor of minors, finds himself relating the
plots of his favorite 1940 romantic films to Valentin, a
heterosexual twenty-four-year-old Marxist-anarchist serving
out a sentence for consipiracy against the present regime.
The reader is thrust into a politically volatile Argentina of
the 1970s, where prisoners are granted pardons by insidious
wardens for spying on their cellmates and revealing their
innermost secret-subversive selves. Most of the book's
sixteen chapters are dialogues between the two men, who
fill in the time as the lights go out every evening with the
fantastic plots of Molina's favorite forties films. As the
dialogues progress the men begin to feel affection for each

other, and the rigidity of their sexual roles disappears.
They make love before Molina leaves prison; Valentin con-
vinces his apolitical cellmate to carry some confidential messages to accomplices within the city.   Molina (who had "co-
operated" with the warden and received a pardon for revealing very little about Valentin) is put under twenty-four-hour
surveillance, and his phones are tapped.   Upon delivering
the clandestine information to Valentin's anti-regime party
members, Molina is shot in a crossfire between the activists
and police.   Valentin is subsequently tortured.   In a stream-
of-consciousness monologue he justifies the death of Molina
and his love for him: "I think he let himself be killed because that way he could die like some heroine in a movie,
and none of that business about a just cause" (p. 279).

At one point in the novel Molina asks Valentin if he
would be repelled if the window dresser just "kissed" him.
And Valentin says, "You're a spiderwoman, that traps men
in her web" (p. 260).   In his last monologue he refers to
Molina as the spiderwoman who wears

> "silver lamé, that fits her like a glove, ... wear-
> ing a [silver] mask ... but ... poor creature ...,
> she can't move, ... trapped in a spider web, ...
> I just feel like sleeping after eating all that food I
> found thanks to the spiderwoman....   What's the
> most difficult thing of all to realize?   That I live
> deep inside your thoughts and so I'll always re-
> main with you, you'll never be alone ... if the
> two of us think the same then we're together ... "
> (pp. 280-281).

In a devastating subplot, Valentin is given doctored
food by the prison to weaken him, so that Molina, in exchange for a parole, would reveal to the warden the anar-
chist's political schemes and the names of other party members.   When the men become very friendly and later intimate, Molina manages to wheedle "gourmet" groceries from
the warden, believing Valentin to be suspicious of the visits
from Molina's mother, who usually brought two bags of food,
food that Molina uses to repair Valentin's failing health.

Puig alternates chapters of dialogue with four monologues by Molina about various, unidentified film scenarios.
Val Lewton's The Cat Woman was certainly the first film;
it is this that cements their reality-fantasy relationship.
Other film plots akin to I Walked with a Zombie, the World

War II drama Paris Underground, and an M-G-M Holiday in
Mexico-type musical drama are presented throughout the
novel and in themselves are quite interesting and well written.
Obviously, Puig's career as a scenarist did not go to waste;
"Cinema in the Novels of Manuel Puig" will probably be the
subject of a future article or doctoral dissertation.

As a counterpoint to the plot and scenarios, nine footnotes are presented, eight of them seriously dealing with the
psychological ramifications of homosexuality; one is written
in the style of a press-book for the "Paris-World War II"
film, portraying the vicissitudes of its leading actress in
making the film.   The reader may prefer to skip over the
footnotes, since they represent the "serious voice" of authority, society, possibly the author.   Perhaps Puig is making
ironical comments on the dialogue.   One critic felt that
"when Molina acknowledges his masculinity and Valentin his
femininity, [it is] a realization of the Utopian theory, expressed in the footnotes, that human society will only become
sane and free when rigid sex-role models are cast off."[25]
Mario Vargas Llosa would embrace Puig were he to read
Chapter Fifteen and the latter's surveillance reports, a great
bit of eclecticism probably taken from Captain Pantoja and
the Special Service.   Cabrera Infante shares Puig's penchant
for relating movies to the feelings of his characters, as in
Three Trapped Tigers.

Puig's strength as a writer rests upon the authenticity
with which he creates his voices and dialogues of his characters.   He demands that readers use their own imaginations
(for example, in the recreation of screenplays), while he, the
novelist, remains absent from the monologue.   "What makes
Puig so fascinating ... is the extraordinary inventiveness he
exhibits in devising new ways to render familiar material."[26]

A true descendant of William Faulkner, Manuel Puig
uses other resources than interior monologue, footnotes,
verbal collages, quasi-cinematic descriptions, even dialogues
in which one person's speech is suppressed, to weave his
very human, sentimental tales.   "Like Nabokov, Puig takes
endless delight in contemporary poshlost--all the most
shameless forms of trash masquerading as sublimity--while
using it against itself to show how it deforms lives and how
a cunningly crafted literary art can transcend it."[27]   Puig
is a camp novelist.   "He has made a literary habit of patch-
ing together his witty, ironic stories out of the clichés and
conventions of popular culture at its trashiest."[28]   If one

were to cite Susan Sontag's fifty-eight points from her 1964
"Notes on Camp," one could correlate and corroborate Puig's
literary aesthetic with this movement, a movement that Puig
doubtlessly fully embraces. To paraphrase Sontag, for Puig,
camp is a sensibility, a vision of the world in terms of
style and innocence, an act that proposes and takes itself
seriously (but really cannot be taken thus), an attempt to do
something extraordinary, glamorous, needing fantasy, the
theatricalization of experience, proposing a comic vision of
the world, playful, anti-serious, a mode of enjoyment, an
appreciation.

        The secrets behind Manuel Puig's successful literary
career are multiple.   Puig's novels were deliberately written
for popular acceptance and accessibility to all levels of society.   He may be "too corny for the sophisticated appetites
of people trained to decipher Borges, Bioy-Casares and
Cortázar, "29 but, as mentioned above, Heartbreak Tango,
for example, sold over a hundred thousand copies in Argentina alone, especially among the blue-collar sector, because
he satisfied a universal hunger for believable romantic fiction.   In fact, what is so "right" about all of Puig's novels
is the rightness of what the characters say in their monologues, dialogues about their real or fantasized world.   Puig
has used the metaphor of the media, especially cinema, to
fine advantage, in some cases to let characters "betray their
genuine selves when they accept films as a frame of refer-
ence. "30   Alfred J. MacAdam writes:

        Puig uses what is immediately available to him,
        but he bends it to his own purpose.   Whether it
        be the motion picture, or serial novel, Puig sug-
        gests there is more to the message through the
        medium, that nostalgia and escapism are possibly
        desired within contemporary society and that the
        brutal portrayal of reality, meager life or a life
        of mediocrity is not his major emphasis as novel-
        ist. 31

Puig, writes John Brushwood, "avoids looking down on his
characters [whose] effect is enhanced ... by the near absence of a narrator.   The activated reader is in direct com-
munication with the character and there is no need for the
author to interpret them. "32   Again, MacAdam: "Puig's in-
visible artist calls attention to himself by his very absence.
He is the final distillation of the realist nineteenth-century
artist-god, everywhere and nowhere, revealing himself

through his stylistic dexterity. "[33]   For the vital "experience"
of reader participation in the book is more valuable to the
reader than the memory of the book itself.   This experience
may be characterized by artificiality, contrivance, by the
very means the narrative is propelled which leaves the reader mentally, but rarely emotionally, stimulated.   For with
all of Puig's experiments, collage-building literary games,
media effects, contrived multiple-storytelling devices, parodies, campiness, the baseness of taste to which his themes
appeal, and unashamedly sentimental plots, "his work is in-
delibly etched, inescapably interesting but impersonal, cold,
utilizing the insidious power of unanalyzed popular culture to
unearth basic unspoken human truths. "[34]   There is a cold,
sterile, laconic factualness in his novels that masks compassion with camp, sentiment with accurate perception.   If
Puig's minor contribution to the Latin American narrative
were exclusively the brilliant possibility of using pop-art
forms, his work would have been a flash of light, quickly
gone from the public scene.   But, writes David Foster, Puig,
avoiding the dense, expressionistic structures of his contemporaries, Cortázar, Vargas Llosa, and Fuentes, "reveals a
sustained control of form ... in the finely achieved atmosphere of reader alienation. "[35]   But alienation from what?

Kiss of the Spiderwoman represents Puig's first unspoken attempt to grapple with the political stranglehold the
government of Argentina exercises over its masses, jailing
those who oppose the regime, casting homosexuals out of
society.   It is perhaps these "alienations" that the author is
addressing.   Puig, however, does not consider his works
political.

> The need for change is so obvious in Latin Amer-
> ica that it is not necessary to have novels spelling
> the fact out.   I doubt if anyone who hasn't already
> been converted to the cause will ever be by peace-
> fulness.   It seems to me anyway that serious
> journalism is far more successful than literature
> in politics. ...   One must not forget that it takes
> about two or three years to write a novel.   At
> the rate that things develop in Latin America, a
> novelist cannot hope to keep pace. [36]

The above was quoted from an interview in Montevideo's
newspaper Marcha in 1972.   This writer believes that Puig
has since changed his mind.   He has always been an implicit
critic of Argentine society, but in Kiss of the Spiderwoman

he explicitly reveals the sad state of the Buenos Aires prison system, the punishments meted out to anarchists, the underlying pathos and fragility of the human condition of the contemporary Argentine. One could easily see why Kiss was banned: for the first time, Puig, with perfect naturalness and spontaneity, deals with the authentic environment of homosexuals and anarchists in prison and the corrupt political system that punishes them.

Of wide appeal to the secretaries, writers, and policemen that appear in them, Puig's books have "achieved a successful balance between sophistication and accessibility. "[37] Because of the wide popularity of his first two novels, The Buenos Aires Affair and Kiss would have been instantaneous best-sellers in Argentina because of their provocative and timely themes. If Kiss had been merely an entertainment, Puig would have ended the novel two chapters earlier, having Valentin and Molina embrace happily as lovers in their final kiss; in the language he used in his retelling of the filmed scenarios, Molina would say "That's all folks. The End. " Puig's addition of the surveillance scene, depicting current-day police methods in the metropolis of Buenos Aires and Valentin's brutal beating leading to his probable death, invest the novel with a political dimension not expressed so graphically in any of Puig's earlier novels. Also unlike his earlier fictions, Kiss of the Spiderwoman is not the usual jumble of truncated structures from which a plot emerges but, rather, a beautifully controlled narrative that skillfully conveys basic human values, a vivid demonstration of the continuing of the genre itself. Manuel Puig is a novelist moving in the direction of political commitment in his depiction of the provincial and urban middle class of Argentina, something that has never before been attempted so successfully in Latin American letters. Clearly, Puig, thriving self-exiled from his native country, is an eclectic stylist, a consummate artist.

9. SARDUY: CUBAN "CAMP"

If Manuel Puig is the Argentine exponent of camp, Severo
Sarduy's fiction is the compleat embodiment of a camp manifesto that never takes anything seriously. It "takes the entire cosmos as its subject, adheres to mutilations and swift
changes and deals with the disintegration and rebirth of the
world. "1 Sarduy's campiness is the embodiment of everything that is playful, humorous, and wildly imaginative.
Some critics consider his works to be the most experimental
and challenging of all Latin American fiction today.   Unlike
Puig, Sarduy does not provide his readers with straightforward storytelling, remarkable insights, or identifiable protagonists.   However, like Puig in his Kiss of the Spiderwoman, Sarduy does glorify the best aspects of camp, create
and explode images and words in an attempt to portray "the
ultimate mutability of human landscapes, "2 a hallucinatory
universe through his own interpretation of surface reality.
Sarduy insists, as did his tutors and fellow celebrants
Lezama Lima and Cabrera Infante, that language--metamor-
phized, transmuted, truncated, or syncretized, with its own
inner logic, its metaphors as celebrations of themselves, --
that language is everything.

Severo Sarduy was born on February 25, 1937, in
Camagüey, Cuba.   Very little is known about his youth and
adolescence.   When asked to write his own chronology, he
commented: "I have no sense of time, I don't understand
the sequence of events nor do they seem to correspond to
precise moments for me.   I don't believe in the idea of
continuity. "3   This should give the reader some notion of
the timeless character of Sarduy's fictions.   At any event,
in 1956 he was sent to Havana to begin studies at the university's medical school.   He had published some early

poems in Ciclón, "a dissident branch of Orígines, edited by
José Rodríguez Feo and livened up by Virgilio Piñera,"4 and
had always wanted to continue his "vocation" as a writer.
As the Castro revolution gained momentum and Fidel made
his official entry into Havana in 1959, Sarduy dropped his
medical studies and wrote some poetry, which appeared in
Diario Libre and Lunes de Revolución.

With a government grant in 1960 Sarduy went to
Europe to study art history.   He also took trips to Caracas,
New York, and Tokyo in pursuit of his studies.   Between
1960 and 1964 he lived mostly in Madrid and Paris, where
he gave courses in the Louvre's School of Art and in the
Sorbonne's School for Advanced Studies, and journeyed
throughout Europe.   It was Franz Kline's action paintings,
"his fascination for the black bars ... over white canvasses
while dancing"5 that inspired his first novel, Gestures (1963),
a book of action writing.

Gestures dealt with a mulatto woman's activities as
theatrical performer and as a partisan activist for the Castro
revolution.   Critics felt that the fragmented, parodic style
was very reminiscent of the French nouveau roman as well
as Kline's "new" action painting.   In 1969 Sarduy began publishing many articles in French; he became associated with
the Tel Quel group of experimental writers, although his
themes were always Cuban.   When he wrote in Spanish, like
Cabrera Infante he preferred the "Cuban" method of express-
ing his themes.   A quick review of his articles will demonstrate Sarduy's prolific and diverse contributions to a variety
of magazines, including the prestigious Tel Quel, Mundo
Nuevo, Sur, La Quinzaine Litteraire, Art Press, and Plural,
as well as his critical participation in books about art, his
prologues, prefaces, epilogues, and introductions to art cata-
logs.

In 1967 literary critic Emir Rodríguez Monegal
rescued Sarduy's second novel, From Cuba with a Song,
after its first rejection in manuscript.   A more experimental
work than Gestures, Cuba presents Sarduy's analysis of
Cuban culture, using the Chinese, African, and Spanish contributions to demonstrate the racial intermingling that defines
the Cuban nation and personality.   Transvestites appear and
disappear in the course of the narrative, imposing a unity
over the diverse sections.   Sarduy's tale is one of drugs,
hallucinations, and eroticism, portrayed in poetic language
that is moving and baroque.   He described his narrative

technique as "a collage that moves inward, made up of poetry, epitaphs, dialogues, activating the reader as the three aspects of Cuban culture become interrelated, deepening the significance of the book."[6]

Returning briefly to the essay, Sarduy composes Written on a Body in 1969, discussing once again his fascination with literature and transvestism, transgression, and eroticism. Monegal writes: "An erotic writer who has discovered the pleasures of the text, Sarduy is today not only the most experimental of Latin American writers but also the one who has completely erased the boundaries between prose and poetry."[7] In 1971 Sarduy wrote a radio script entitled The Beach, which was presented in Stuttgart, Germany, as well as two moderately successful books of poems, Flamenco and Mood Indigo. Other plays conceived in Sarduy's "theatre of immobility" concept and presented in Stuttgart were Departure and The Fall. It was not until 1972 that he became known internationally for his famous third novel Cobra, which was first published in France. Cobra won the Medicis Prize for Literature in 1972. It also led him to write another essay, Baroque (1974), which tries to link the roots of baroque art to the scientific discoveries of Newton, Galileo, and Kepler. In Cobra, Sarduy began to show fascination for the "rhetorical" figure of the ellipse. To quote Emir Rodríguez Monegal once again: "What [Sarduy] has found is not the certainty of a God, placed solidly in the center of the universe, as in Lezama, but the certainty of the void created by an elliptical system with one empty center."[8]

In 1973 Severo Sarduy made a tour of the East, visiting Singapore and Jakarta. He worked for French National Television in Paris in 1974 and wrote a weekly television and radio program Science in France. In the same year another book of poetry, Big-Bang, appeared, published while Sarduy was working on his fourth novel. Also in 1974 he returned to the Far East, visiting Turkey, Iran, and other places. Presently living in Paris, Sarduy in 1977 finished Maitreya, a kind of anti-Cobra, which was brought out in Spain the following year. Probably his most experimental work to date, Maitreya has as its theme mysticism, the role of the Buddha, and the double. The book capitalizes upon the parodies of language the author had attempted in his earlier novels and provides the reader with the word plays, palimpsets, erotic prose, and baroque stylistics for which Sarduy has come to be known.[9]

Cobra is a short but complex work that defies complete analysis.   So much has been written about it, pro and
con, especially about its phantasmagorical, phenomenological,
and linguistic aspects, that it is difficult to write a single,
simple opinion about Sarduy's life and art.   Let us turn to
Cobra itself, its plot and its style, and then try to appraise
it in light of the current resurgence of the Latin American
narrative.

Cobra is organized into two sections.   In Part One
the protagonist Cobra is a transvestite, the star of a theater
troupe somewhere in Europe or the chief prostitute in the
Great Lyrical Theatre of Dolls, a brothel.   Cobra may be
female in the first part and male in the second, depending
upon the use of the pronouns "he" and "she."   She was created in Part One from a wax doll by Madame and resides in
the brothel with other dolls named Dior, Cadillac, and Sontag who are jealous when she becomes Queen of the Lyrical
Theatre.   The "doll," however, becomes humanized, and
Cobra tells Madame: "Why did you bring me into the world
if it wasn't absolutely divine?"   She demands a sex change.
One evening s(he) discovers a White Dwarf named Pup, her
self-image.   Cobra moves in a world of theatricals, among
Madame (who perhaps created her), the stud Estuchio, and
Pup, who encourages her (his) transformation or conversion
by a mysterious Dr. Ktazob.   The doctor is finally found in
a North African slum, probably in an abortion clinic somewhere in Tangiers, where he ritualistically "kills" and then
revives Cobra in her (his) new form, probably as a male.

In Part Two we are probably in Paris at Le Drug-
store, where Cobra takes up with a motorcycle gang and is
summarily tortured, raped, and killed in a kinky religious
ceremony by Tundra, Scorpio, Totem, and Tiger as they
move on to Amsterdam.   All the motorcyclists are in search
of their own identity; a Guru in Amsterdam sets them on a
path to India, where they attend some complex, cosmic funeral ceremony, and Cobra is united with Nirvana or the elusive Hindu God Shiva or some such diety.

> May the lotus flower
> be, by the Diamond joined (p. 176).

The lotus symbolizes regeneration and is joined to the diamond or mystical center of Cobra's universe. [10]

Sarduy admits to finding the inspiration for his novel

in a real event.   Apparently, Cobra was a transvestite in a
Parisian cabaret called Carousel who was actually killed in
an air crash on Mt. Fujiyama as his (her) troupe was returning to Paris.   Sarduy then met one of Cobra's lovers,
who told the author about his (her) passion for physical perfection and achieving the absolute. [11]   Enough said about
Sarduy's "inspiration."

The novel's style is strange, alien to anything this
writer has ever encountered by a Latin American novelist.
In an amusing footnote, Sarduy himself says:

> Moronic reader: if even with these clues, thick
> as posts, you have not understood that we're deal-
> ing with a metamorphosis of the painter of the
> preceding chapter ... [then] abandon this novel and
> devote yourself to screwing or to reading the nov-
> els of the Boom, which are much easier (p. 42).

Sarduy's style is precious, pretentious, neo-baroque,
gay, self-mocking, campy, and heavy.   Like Puig, he de-
lights in cinematic references and footnotes, and takes camp
and trashiness for his themes.   The following paragraph, a
description of Cobra after a "performance," gives one an
idea of Sarduy's style.

> The itch gnawed at her--"pernicious leprosy";
> as soon as the canned applause would explode she'd
> run into the wings--she had sunk to those therapeutic
> depths--to splash in a bowl of ice.   She would put
> on the imperial cothurnuses again and return to
> the stage, fresh as a cucumber.   To these thermic
> surprises the invaders responded with great ma-
> neuvers: from her nails a vascular violet burst
> out which smacked of frozen orchid, of an asthmat-
> ic bishop's cloak: beneath a crumbling refectory
> he eats a pineapple.
> That Lezamesque purple was followed by cracks
> in her ankles, hives, and then abscesses rising
> from between her toes, dark green sores on her
> soles (p. 19).

Notice Sarduy's homage to Lezama Lima, whose disciple he
once was, and his attention to surfaces, use of spectacular
adjectival constructions, and violent colors.   Sarduy's portrayal of events in Cobra, writes Suzanne Jill Levine, "suggests that history is fiction, life is theater, a place is a

textual painting."12 Cobra's theme is that life is pure
theater, and as in a theater, the only true realities lie on
the surfaces of its text, which is "a playful series of trans-
mutations,"13 a protean exercise for author and reader alike.

Within the novel Sarduy seems to present his own
manifesto for writing, especially in Part One: "Writing is
the art of ellipsis, the art of digression, the art of recreat-
ing reality, the art of restoring history, the art of disorgan-
izing an order and organizing a disorder, the art of patchwork [bricolage]." These pronouncements are repeated
throughout the novel, reaffirming to us (and perhaps to Sarduy) his own intentions.

It is easy to lose the continuity of Cobra's plot,
since much of the novel is clouded by esoterica, a constant
return to the "teddy-boy" leather-jacket, motorcycle-gang
philosophy of the 1950s (which may appear somewhat decadent
and recherché in the 1970s), and a host of anagrams, puns,
and surreal images (like flowers sprouting from motorbikes).
Readers are grateful for Sarduy's occasional footnotes, especially the one that defines the multiple meanings of
"Cobra": a poisonous snake in India; a motorcycle gang
near St. Germain des Près; a group of artists centered in
Copenhagen, Brussels, and Amsterdam; the singer who died
in a plane crash over Mt. Fujiyama; and the receipt of
wages, from the Spanish verb cobrar. Footnotes such as
these help readers decode Cobra's reality, as they move
through a narcotic-hazed theatrical world of whores, motorcycle freaks, pretentious Indian mystics, and erratic sym-
bols. According to Levine:

> In Cobra, ultimate reality is Sarduy's language
> focused on the significant value of each word skill-
> fully manipulating signs and figures ..., giving the
> surface and iconography of Cobra a worth both
> cultural and social. The text not only signifies in
> the traditional sense, but also helps to decode a
> reality without presuming to exhaust its meanings.14

I have deliberately avoided dealing with various critical interpretations of Cobra: Roland Barthes's utopic praise
of the book in his Pleasures of the Text, Claude Lévi-
Strauss's notion of "writing as bricolage" (patchwork), Rodríguez Monegal's effort to prove that Cobra is a text of continual metamorphosis, Sarduy's reading of Octavio Paz's
images of India in his text or the references to Jacques

Derrida or Lacan's hidden presence or Julia Kristeva's read-
ing of Bakhtine on Sarduy's notion of parody and Lezama
Lima's interpretation of the baroque and his influence on
Sarduy as manifested in Cobra.

Cobra is a Fellini-esque, theatrical, and cinematic
spectacular, heavily influenced by the French nouveau roman,
or anti-novel. Although it expresses its own theories of
literature, it is very difficult to determine if it is an "entertainment" or a serious work in light of its own heavy baroqueness, its grammatical and syntactical connotations, its mean-
ingless, incomprehensible passages. Cobra is a manipulated
work, totally fabricated as the language Sarduy uses. "His
sentences surprise; the rhythms confound and startle us, and
exhaust us, with a frightened beauty...."[15] Sarduy is the
master of wordscapes that dip, shake, and explode.

Cobra has been considered a dazzling performance,
tantalizing, kaleidoscopic, Brechtian, elliptical, in constant
flux. "Sarduy's novels, " writes Rodríguez Monegal, "are constructed with the rigor and fantasy of poems. They are devoted not to the construction of narrative (like those of Vargas Llosa) but to the 'deconstruction' of language."[16] Cobra
is ironic, parodic, macabre, bizarre, strange, mercurial,
inscrutable, enigmatic, a travesty, an orgy, a nightmare,
provocative, vertiginous, delirious, carnivalesque, trashy,
controversial, camp. It has been compared to William Bur-
roughs's American cult classic novel Naked Lunch--probably
because it is also a "naked" book demanding a "naked" response. This writer agrees with Robert M. Adams, who
writes: "Cobra is a glossy, evasive book, from which this
reader emerged chiefly with a deep sense of astral chill."[17]
There are scenes of sadism told with stylistic baroque ele-
gance, shrill "chills of intergalactic space, which the baroque
stylistics only deepen."[18] S. J. Levine writes: "Cobra, the
snake, the actress, the verb, the symbol of a pictorial school
is the novel ... an infinite play (within its finite nature) of
transformations and repetitions branching from the vocable
"cobra" as it winds its way along its slippery, rootless
route."[19] "Cobra, " writes reviewer Jerome Charnyn, "is
crafty, slippery and poisonous."[20]

Although Sarduy has borrowed much from the experimental nouveau roman and remains faithful to his own tropical setting of Cuba's myths, colors, movements, and violence,
he remains a hermetic stylist and a writer whose works are
simply not to everybody's taste. Like Manuel Puig, he is

omniscient, detached, almost alienated from his own fiction, but with his intrusive footnotes, he lets us admire his tour de force. However, unlike Puig's, his plots are distorted and dictated by phonetic associations or by the internal logic of language itself. Because of Sarduy's "astral" coldness, there exists for this reader a void that baroque stylistics and linguistic dalliance cannot fulfill no matter how original, fantastic, creative, or playful.

10. DONOSO: CHILEAN PHANTASMAGORIA

If Severo Sarduy's novels may be considered "coldly elusive," José Donoso's are "boldly hallucinogenic." Somewhat
paradoxically, Sarduy has enhanced the reputation of both
Puig and Donoso in articles for several well-known literary
magazines.[1] Where Sarduy called attention to the "rightness" of language in Manuel Puig's novels, he demonstrates
how Donoso captures outward appearances from the "inside,"
through the "rightness" of his own verbal world.

Donoso's novels do not primarily describe places,
events, and characters from the outside, but cram all of
these elements into worlds of words, a world aware of its
own verbal nature. More often than not his novels are complex and his characters fragmented and difficult to identify
or distinguish from one another whether through their own
dialogues or channeled through the consciousness of a narrator. Donoso's greatest gifts are his glorious flights of
imagination, the frank revelation of his consciousness, the
portrayal of his aesthetic sensations, and his profound insights into the realities elucidated through his startling prose.
Language is the center of Donoso's novels, and Donoso aban-
dons traditional plot, character, and thematic development in
order to depict today's world in his own meaningful, spontaneous way, much in the spirit of the anti-novelists.

There has been much critical controversy over his
most celebrated novel, The Obscene Bird of Night, usually
associated with the "boom" of the "new" Latin American
narrative. Bird has been characterized as "a giant Thalid-
omide novel filled with grotesques, a delirious non-stop flight
of the imagination, monstrous because as Baudelaire said,
'all beauty is bizarre,' miraculous because the book issues

100

from a writer immensely neglected here [in the United States.]"[2]   It is safe to generalize that in the world of José Donoso, all is not what it seems.

Bird is a novel that is, in reality, a long monologue spoken by a deaf and dumb man, Mudito/Humberto, who was once secretary to Don Jerónimo de Azcoitía, a rich land-owner, one of whose properties is a squalid Catholic retreat populated by orphans, cripples, and beggar women.   What-ever milieu Donoso is describing, his theme is always Chile and its society.   "Bird," writes Philip Ward, "deals with this theme in a vivid, surrealist language and concentrates on the atmosphere of decay, despair and delirium which Donoso clearly identifies with the world he lives in in one of the most powerful novels to emerge from Latin Ameri-ca."[3]   In the words of Emir Rodríguez Monegal, "It abolish-es the conventions of time and place, individual identity and authorial point of view.   Close in tone to Hieronymous Bosch or to Luis Buñuel's dream sequences, this book is Donoso's masterpiece."[4]

Donoso admits to having been influenced by novelists from countries other than his own--Fuentes, Cortázar, Carpentier, and most certainly Faulkner, Lawrence, James, Proust, Joyce, and Wolfe.[5]   It was also North America's sponsorship of the "boom" of the Latin American novel that brought Donoso's Obscene Bird to readers here, not express-ly because of its own extraordinary style but perhaps because of the exotic element in his fiction.   As Paul West has put it, "The North American literary sensibility thrives on con-tiguous exotophily, not on taste, respect for innovation or distinguished style."[6]   Donoso's susceptibility to literary in-fluence makes the style evolved in Obscene Bird and subse-quent works impossible to label as "authentically" Chilean. In fact, Donoso has had a particularly nomadic existence, leading one critic to believe that "he sounds like a man with-out a country or a history of his own,"[7] an exile who lost his tongue.

José Donoso was born on October 5, 1924, in Santiago, Chile.   He was the first child of Dr. José Donoso, a young physician more addicted to horse racing and cards than to his profession, and Alicia Yáñez, a pretty, amusing woman who somehow coped.[8]   Two brothers were born in subse-quent years, Gonzalo in 1927 and Pablo in 1931, as the Donoso family moved to live with his father's great-aunts. When José was eight years old he entered The Grange, an

English day school, and remained there unhappily until 1943.
While there, however, he read the accepted children's classics of Verne and Dumas and became interested in the more
fashionable novelists, such as Somerset Maugham, Aldous
Huxley, Pearl Buck, and Margaret Mitchell. As a teenager
he went to the beach and the movies but his conduct was un-
manageable. "I continued to play hookey, spending days on
the outskirts of Santiago talking to derelicts of various sorts.
Gradually I faded away from school. "9 Never completing his
bachillerato, Donoso officially dropped out of school; he
worked in a travel agency and at a multitude of jobs before
buying a third-class ticket on a steamer bound for the Straits
of Magellan.

        In 1945 he landed at Punto Arenas and worked his way
up on the Argentine pampas as a shepherd. He hitchhiked
from Patagonia to Buenos Aires working as a dock hand but
came down with the measles in 1946. His family took him
back home to Santiago in 1947; there he finally finished his
bachillerato and enrolled in the University of Chile, specializ-
ing in English studies, "not an approved career for an upper
middle class boy in those days in Chile. "10 In 1949 Donoso
received a Doherty Foundation Scholarship to study English
at Princeton University, was delighted with his studies in
literature there, and published his first two short stories,
"The Blue Woman" and "The Poisoned Pastries, " in MSS,
a Princeton Literary Review. In 1951 he received his
Bachelor of Arts degree and hitchhiked throughout the United
States, Mexico, and Central America.

        Returning home to Chile in 1952, he taught English at
the Kent School and the Pedagological Institute of the University of Santiago. His childhood "stomach" pains also returned, and Donoso went into psychoanalysis, which may have
helped him. In 1954 he wrote his first short story in Spanish, "China, " and a year later his first complete book of
short stories, Summertime and Other Stories, was published,
earning for him the Santiago Municipal Short Story Prize.
Donoso recalled that he and his friends had to hawk the book
on trolleys to turn a slight profit. In 1957 Donoso left teaching and went to live with a fisherman's family in Isla Negra
to complete his first novel Coronation (1957). That year
marked his first experience with a hemorrhaging ulcer, which
caused him to black out. Between 1958 and 1960 Donoso,
true to his nomadic nature, borrowed some money and set
out for a tour of South America. After visiting Pablo Neruda,
Chile's Nobel Prize-winning poet, he reached Buenos Aires,

spent two years there, and met María del Pilar Serrano, a
sophisticated painter to whom he became engaged and whom he
married in 1961.   In 1959 he published several short stories:
"Footsteps in the Night, " "The Closed Door, " and "Paseo";
The Charleston and Other Short Stories, a book-length col-
lection of new and previously published stories, also appeared.
Donoso became a reporter for the weekly newsmagazine
Ercilla at about this time.

         In 1962 Donoso wrote another short story, "Santelices, "
and began to lecture in the College of Journalism at the University of Chile.   He also became the editor of Ercilla and
the magazine's leading literary critic.   Attending a Writer's
Conference at the University of Concepción in Chile, he first
met Carlos Fuentes, relating to him the nucleus of a plot
idea for a novel that later became The Obscene Bird of
Night.   In 1963 Coronation won the Faulkner Foundation
Prize for the best postwar Chilean novel, and Alfred Knopf
agreed to publish it in English.   Donoso also began writing
"The Last Azcotía, " a story that was to grow into Obscene
Bird; this coincided with a recurrence of his ulcer pains.
In 1964 Donoso and his wife left for Mexico to attend the
Writer's Conference at Chichén-Itzá; in 1965 Knopf published
The Best Short Stories of José Donoso, containing fourteen
of his previously published shorter pieces.   Also in 1965 he
spent some time in Mexico City, where he wrote the novella
Hell Without Limits in Carlos Fuentes's garden (as the latter
was writing A Change of Skin in his study), did some literary
criticism for Siempre, and published his second novel, This
Sunday, hemorrhaging with his second ulcer attack as he
completed the last chapter of this novel.

         Deciding to take a break from writing, Donoso ac-
cepted a job teaching creative writing in English at the University of Iowa's Writer's Workshop between 1965 and 1967.
"While English would always be his second language, " writes
Rodríguez Monegal, "the whole of his literary production
would be in Spanish.   Donoso, unlike Nabokov or Beckett,
was not destined to become an expatriate, using an adopted
language as his medium in place of his native tongue."11
However, because he wanted to continue with Obscene Bird,
he quit his job ("writing was evidently incompatible with
teaching"12) and moved to Mallorca with his wife and newly
adopted daughter born in Madrid.   That same year, 1967,
This Sunday was published in English as well as another
short story, "Ana María. "   Donoso was becoming a hypo-
chondriac, and at his wife's suggestion he consulted a psy-
chiatrist.

Unable to continue with Obscene Bird for two years, in 1969 he became guest editor for two issues of Tri-Quarterly, the American magazine devoted to Latin American letters, and lectured briefly at Colorado State University, where a bleeding ulcer forced him to undergo emergency surgery. "Due to my ability to tolerate pain killers," the author recalls vividly, "I was mad for a few days, with hallucinations, split personality, paranoia and suicide attempts."[13] Returning to Spain from Mallorca, the Donosos regrouped in Barcelona, where the aftereffects of the author's madness took a couple of years to disappear. He began rewriting Obscene Bird while still suffering from nightmares and paranoia, completed it by the end of 1970, and submitted the manuscript to the Seix Barral Company for its Biblioteca Breve Prize. Although it did not win the coveted literary prize because of censorship problems (about some ten to twelve lines had to be changed in all), the Bird was launched by its publisher and was immediately translated into French. Exhausted with all of Bird's activities, Donoso and his family left Barcelona for Calaceite in Teruel, southwest of the Catalonian capital, where they moved into a seventeenth-century stone house, which had to be completely refurbished.

In 1971, after spending some five thousand dollars repairing his country home, Donoso saw the publication of Stories, a group of fourteen of his best short works. The following year Donoso turned to the essay and wrote The Boom in Spanish-American Literature: A Personal History (1972). His novella Hell Has No Limits appeared in English in an edition containing novellas by Fuentes and Sarduy. The move to Calaceite had been favorable to Donoso's health and career. Apart from his essay on the "boom," another group of novellas appeared in 1973 entitled Sacred Families. The year 1973 was a critical one for Donoso's career. The Obscene Bird of Night was published in English to mostly outstanding reviews, and Donoso received his second prestigious Guggenheim Award (the first was received in 1968), which helped him to finish Sacred Families and complete his latest novel, Country House, published in Spain in late 1978 but still untranslated as of this writing.

Late in 1973 Donoso was preparing to return to Chile when a military coup there forced him to cancel his trip. In 1975, after lecturing for a short while at Princeton University, he returned to his homeland but found the new political regime so oppressive that he exiled himself to Spain,

never to return.   In 1976 he and his family moved to Sitges,
a small Catalonian resort town on Spain's Costa Brava,
where he finished writing Country House.   In 1978 Donoso's
Personal History of the Boom,   Charleston and Other Stories,
and Sacred Families all appeared simultaneously in English
in North America.   Donoso currently remains in self-
imposed exile, his nomadic existence temporarily suspended
until he recoups his health and completes his latest writing
project.

José Donoso is now at the peak of his career.   When
The Obscene Bird of Night was published in 1970, it was
also at the peak of the "boom" years when the literary movement in Latin America began its decline.   Donoso's own
analysis of the "boom's" fizzle makes interesting reading,
since the split over the Seix Barral award for 1970 was one
of the factors that led to his disillusionment with the movement.   Fidel Castro's arrest of Cuban poet Herberto Padilla
caused a rift among many of the "boom" movement's leftist
literati.   Critic Emir Rodríguez Monegal, who had supported
the literary "boom," identified its chief source as the
Cuban revolution, whose leftist and socialist support gained
the literary movement many supporters and fomented the
artificial growth of interest in the Latin American novel.
But for all this blend of political intrigue, artifice, and
editorial chicanery, it is essentially because of Donoso and
the other nine writers under scrutiny in this volume that
the Latin American narrative is indeed alive and well and
has aided the careers of many new and younger writers.
Donoso himself made the following appraisal of his own contributions to the Latin American narrative:

> The "boom" has been a game; perhaps more pre-
> cisely, a broth which for a decade nourished the
> outmoded form of the novel in Latin America, and
> the "boom" will disappear--already, it is spoken
> of less--and there will remain three or four or
> five outstanding novels which will remind us of it
> and because of which all this noise and publicity
> will have been worthwhile. [14]

One of the outstanding novels Donoso speaks of is
assuredly his own controversial masterpiece, The Obscene
Bird of Night, a book that has certainly received much critical overexposure.   Known for its nightmarish, surrealistic
images, its diffuse and haphazard stylistics, its ambiguities
and jagged, assymetrical structural design, Bird falls well

into the category of anti-novel, a book in which chronological
time is obliterated by the extended use of interior monologue,
where flashbacks and dynamic movements within the protagonist's psyche result in his final madness, disintegration, and
disappearance, all somewhat resembling elements of Donoso's
own illnesses.   G. R. McMurray writes:

> Brilliant, baffling and haunting, The Obscene Bird
> of Night ... achieves new levels of contact with
> reality by probing, scrutinizing, and extolling ...
> the mysterious, uncharted depths of the human
> psyche.   For this reason, it can be described as
> a monumental, masterfully orchestrated tribute to
> consciousness. [15]

Students of literature will puzzle over Obscene Bird
for years to come, but this chapter will discuss a later
work of Donoso's, Sacred Families, a lesser phantasmagorical world, one characterized by a more traditional technique
and also more in the realm of straightforward storytelling:
an "anti-anti-novel," if you will, a form that perhaps marks
the new direction for Latin American novelists and narratives
for the 1980s.

A shorter, less dense work than Obscene Bird,
Sacred Families has had little critical exposure in the
United States and abroad and is worthy of scrutiny.   Although the novel is set in Barcelona, Donoso is perennially
concerned "with unraveling all the threads that compose the
fabric of Chilean society, "[16] in Monegal's words.   All of
his works, whether written in Chile or in exile, deal explicitly with Chilean life of the twentieth century.   Donoso's
themes are fairly constant throughout his fictions: the alienation, spiritual and emotional disintegration, and rebellious
nature of his protagonists.   Sacred Families is a series of
three novellas (or one longer novel utilizing the same characters) that explicitly treats the theme of possessive materialism within the lives of three urban haute-bourgeois protagonists: a doctor, a dentist, and a model.   The novellas are
not only linked thematically, but certain characters weave in
and out of the fabric of the intrigue that is set primarily in
contemporary Barcelona.

Chattanooga-Choo-Choo is a flight of fantasy narrated
by Anselmo, a doctor-artist-playboy, who sleeps one night
with model Sylvia Corday.   Sylvia's husband Ramón, an

architect, assembles and reassembles his wife, providing
her with new face masks in his own quest for sexual domin-
ation of women.   After a party one night Sylvia and Anselmo
sleep together clandestinely, and in some quirky, surrealist
maneuvering, Sylvia dismantles Anselmo's genitals with vanishing cream, taking revenge on him and her husband for
using her sexually.   Disturbed that his wife Magdalena might
discover his missing member, Anselmo despairs until his
next meeting with Sylvia.   The wives, however, also have
the power to dismember their men.   At the conclusion of
the novella Sylvia tells Magdalena that an error has occurred
... she has Anselmo's "package" and Magdalena has Ramón's.
The women then reassemble their respective husbands, complete with missing parts; the men then reenact the 1940s
song "Chattanooga-Choo-Choo" in a parody of the Andrews
Sisters begun by Sylvia and Magdalena at the party a few
nights before.

        Donoso here is critical of male domination and female
submissiveness, resulting in a pro-Women's Liberation tale
told in surrealistic terms.   His portrait of a haute bourgeoisie that replaces religious values and moral convictions with
easy love, sex, drugs, camp, the gay scene and ventures
into superficial nostalgia, is complete.   Donoso is a master
at mood, creating a sensuous atmosphere that pervades the
entire tale.   He also has a sharp eye and critical ear for
the shallow, hypocritical repartee at the parties reeking with
synthetic atmosphere.   Most fascinating is the grotesque
world he creates, as the reader always waits for the unexpected to happen, in this case, husbands dismantling their
spouses and packing them and their private parts away.
Perhaps commenting on the state of the Latin American novel, Anselmo (Donoso) says at one point: "This sort of thing
(vanishing sex organs) didn't happen except in modern novels
by tropical writers" (p. 36)--an allusion to Sarduy's Cobra?
And describing the participation of a drunk Latin American
writer at a Barcelona party, Donoso once more comments
on an incident:

> But when the publisher suggested that the Latin
> American's novel wasn't selling because the novel
> per se was finished as a literary form, the Latin
> American ... picked up the publisher....   The
> two furious men, each [had their] hands around the
> other's throat....   "The novel form is finished be-
> cause it suits you to have it finished!" (p. 68).

Donoso's peripheral commentary on the end of the "boom."

Green Atom Number Five, another tale of dismember-
ment and disintegration, deals with friends of Anselmo and
Magdalena, Roberto and Marta Ferrer, an older, childless
couple, apparently well adjusted, who are transformed gro-
tesquely into a pair of snarling savages because of a series
of thefts that leave them materialistically and spiritually
bankrupt.   Roberto, a successful dentist, with his wife Marta
decides to buy the "definitive" apartment and fill it with
their own possessions culled and collected over fifteen years
of marriage.   Roberto's own painting, entitled "Green Atom
No. 5," is stolen almost immediately by the porter's brother.
Then an English silver candelabrum disappears.   Light bulbs
and gold ball-point pens are missing.   Paperweights are
stolen by a group of four Seventh Day Adventists trying to
convert the couple to Christ.   Anselmo and Magdalena try
to help the unfortunate couple, but accidents and thefts per-
sist daily.   Marta loses her little finger in an auto accident
as she and Roberto try to stop delivery men from stealing a
Japanese-styled cabinet given to the couple by her mother
many years before.   Flashlights, ashtrays, also disappear.
Mrs. Presen, who takes care of the model Sylvia Corday
and her household, goes off with the Waring Blender.   Paolo,
the gay decorator and party reveler at Ramón's house a few
nights before, watches the apartment's total but slow disintegration.   In a wild cab ride after looking for the stolen painting at the strange address of Pounds-Ounces 204 (probably
indicating the painting's weight) Roberto and Marta strip the
cab driver and finally themselves, reducing each other to a
bestial, violent, and totally nude state.

Certainly, this surrealistic parable à la Cortázar recalls Alain Robbe-Grillet's obsessions with inanimate objects; Donoso depicts what happens to two people who have
always led orderly lives and the consequences of dispossess-
sion, pretentiousness, and sexual sterility.   Anatole Broyard
writes: "The couple are helpless to oppose this despoilation,
have surrendered their sense of self and have nothing left
with which to resist."[17]   An omniscient novelist, Donoso
dissolves the tale, leaving the childless, despoiled couple in
absolute nakedness and despair.   Their physical disintegration also signifies their psychic and moral decay, since
Donoso believes that material objects cannot fulfill or be
used as substitutes for real feelings even with the labyrinth
we know as materialistic society.   Donoso also points out
that--in the words of G. R. McMurray--"the horror of man's
rigidly ordered reality ... is surpassed only by his horror
of chaos as shown by the frightening disintegration that follows the disappearance of Roberto's painting."[18]

Donoso's final novella, <u>Gaspard de la Nuit</u>, receives
its name from Maurice Ravel's famous musical work and re-
unites Sylvia Corday (who had made Anselmo's sex organ
vanish and sang "Chattanooga-Choo-Choo") with Paolo, the
gay decorator, celebrant at Anselmo's house, designer of
Roberto and Marta Ferrer's vanished apartment, and reveler
at other parties given by Barcelona's haute bourgeoisie.
<u>Gaspard</u> relates the story of a teenage boy, Mauricio, visit-
ing his now divorced (reassembled) mother, Sylvia Corday,
the current mistress of Raimundo del Solar.   Mauricio rejects all of her efforts toward reconciliation and occupies
himself by whistling the melody of the title by Ravel.
Donoso's tale reminded one critic of Franz Kafka's "Jose-
phine the Songstress," "a thin echo."[19]   "Music is to young
Mauricio," wrote another reviewer, "what fashion is to
Sylvia and what the perfect apartment is to Roberto and
Marta: a way of erasing the outside world."[20]   Similar to
<u>The Obscene Bird of Night</u>, <u>Gaspard</u> moves us once again
into the world of schizophrenia.   In what is probably the
most complex of the three novellas in this collection (but
not necessarily the most likable), Donoso returns to brilliant storytelling, pulling out all the stops in an effort to
create another short, perceptively psychological masterpiece dealing with the themes of conformity and fantasy.

   <u>Gaspard</u> is a tale of psychic rebellion.   Mauricio
(named after Ravel, he says) tunes out the Barcelona high
life with his frequent trips to the zoo at Villvidrera, re-
fuses offers of a stereo, a Vespa motorbike, hippie shirts,
and amulets to the chagrin of his fashionable but selfish and
desperate mother, anxious to go away to the country or
beach with her lover and not be saddled with her sixteen-
year-old son.   Organized into five sections, Mauricio has a
history of abject loneliness, having been raised mostly by
his grandmother and absentee wealthy father in Madrid.   In
subsequent sections we see Maurice, now on vacation with
his mother in Barcelona, unable to make contact with
"Jackie-O," a woman wheeling a baby carriage who wears
sunglasses in the Kennedy mode.   Next Mauricio is followed
by a brown-suited older man, who, identifying the melody of
<u>Gaspard</u> through Mauricio's whistling, sends the youth fleeing
from a homosexual encounter.   Mauricio's happiest moments
come in the Villvidrera Park area, where he makes contact
with a co-ed group of Catalonian teenagers playing soccer, a
beetle (shades of Kafka), and a supposed raggedy street urchin, his exact double, with whom he evidently changes roles.
And Donoso leaves us with a supposed prince-and-the-pauper
denoument.

What is fascinating about this novella is Donoso's ambiguous ending.   Is the street urchin really there or is he a figment of Mauricio's schizoid personality?   When the new Mauricio arrives home,   he integrates perfectly into Sylvia Corday's lifestyle,   perhaps fulfilling the wishes of the lighter side of his nature.   What is disturbing, however, is Donoso's clinging to the notion of a darker side of Mauricio's personality,   assuming an identity that went against his nature. Ravel's music is the link between Mauricio's abject loneliness ("He was only able to erase all that momentarily when he whistled ... " [p. 191]) and his quest for a new, totally schizophrenic personality ("Instead,   he would go down the other side ... where nobody knew him,   and he would keep walking,   toward other things" [p. 206]).

Gaspard remains an enigma, the tale of a mental depressive,   perhaps anorexic,   whose personality split reveals ambivalent urges to dominate and destroy,   which are,   in reality,   perhaps an individual's reaction to social conformity and crass materialism,   the values of the upper middle class in today's Barcelona (or Santiago).

Despite the many details that place the novellas in Barcelona of the 1970s,   the setting for Sacred Families could be anywhere.   Again, McMurray:

> Universal in its thematic content and often visual in its approach,   this imaginative triptych is the most recent publication to date by a writer whose fundamental message of disillusionment and despair is softened by an acute sense of artistry and a sprinkling of sharp-edged wit,   playfulness and fantasy. [21]

Unlike The Obscene Bird of Night, Sacred Families represents a traditionally story-oriented performance by Donoso, with tightly controlled events leading to unexpected climaxes, somewhat equivalent to the cinematic achievement of his friend Luis Buñuel's The Discreet Charm of the Bourgeoisie, a film that Sacred Families parallels in its "surreal revenge on the worldly and their goods. "[22]   R. Z. Sheppard concluded his review of the novel with these interesting comments: "Donoso balances lean,   graceful prose with a sense of the psychological arabesque.   It is a fine combination for modern ghost stories in which the reader may recognize phantoms of himself. "[23]

Donoso has used his talent and ingenuity, his sense

of surrealism and satire to put a new face on the literature
of disintegration.   All of his fictional works deal with characters who pass fragmented lives or are unable to communi-
cate or are trapped by a conformist society or who suffer
mental, emotional, spiritual, psychic, or geographical isolation.   Donoso identifies these psychological problems for his
readers.   Kessel Schwartz writes: "As Donoso examines the
relationships of poor and rich, he gives the impression that
he is a Chilean combination of Charles Dickens and Henry
James."24   Donoso's view of the human condition may be so
dark and pessimistic that he might also be called the Balzac
of Chilean letters--Balzac, because Donoso's works give us
a broad canvas of society, the violent underside of a conventional bourgeois world that is his perennial theme.   Emir
Rodríguez Monegal has given the most succinct appraisal of
Donoso's career:

> Rather than boring comparison between Donoso and
> Latin American novelists of more epic scope ...,
> I would prefer to link him with the writers who
> have succeeded in transforming the story and their
> lives into fiction, their personal obsessions into
> myths, their terrors and lucid dreams into imagin-
> ative reality, their inner universe into a land
> through which ... the creations of their invention
> move....   There is enough evidence to claim the
> presence of a profound reality in these novels and
> stories of Donoso's....   Because that is where one
> can find the reasons for the profoundly disturbing
> and original nature of the creation of this Chilean
> novelist, who is just now approaching full matur-
> ity. 25

Jos é Donoso, self-proclaimed nomad and exile, at
age fifty-six has just finished his latest novel, Country House,
in Spain.   The book was published there in November of 1978
and was due to be translated into English for publication by
Alfred Knopf some time in 1980.   Donoso's fiction, projected
beyond his native Chile, has elevated his career--and those
of some of his fellow Chilean novelists--to international perspective.   But it is Donoso himself, because of his insight-
ful, stylistically deft prose, who has achieved recognition of
universal stature.

CONCLUSION

The "boom" in Latin American fiction is over. Most of the émigré novelists discussed in this book are still searching for their roots, to clarify their particular national identities and the political, social, and moral issues of their respective countries of origin. The effects of the Cuban revolution and other political upheavals that helped spark the explosion in the Latin American narrative have left countless nomads, exiles, and émigrés uprooted, disturbed, disoriented. Where most writers were leftists before, committed to Fidel Castro's Communist ideology, with its dream to elevate the Cuban people, the majority now have turned from their militant pro-Castro positions. The clouds are still settling after the revolutionary and ideological boom. Although the political scene of Latin America is as baffling as ever, the ideological one has come into clear focus, because the Latin American narrative is very much alive and is doing extremely well.

With Lezama Lima dead, Carpentier is the only Castro supporter left of the Cuban group, writing a historical tribute to the revolution, Año '59 (Year 1959) while residing in Paris from time to time as Cuban ambassador. Fellow Cuban Cabrera Infante resides in London, bitterly attacking the regime he once so loyally supported, and Sarduy has found his own "campy" niche in the Tel Quel world of Parisian literati, as he continues to explore the anti-novel with its bizarre and homosexual themes. The Argentine Cortázar also continues to live and work in Paris, polishing off one group of short stories after another but still living off Hopscotch's reputation. The same could be said of Donoso, self-exiled in Catalonia, as he too lives off the fat of his success with The Obscene Bird of Night, occasionally

112

supported by grants to further his writing pursuits.   Vargas
Llosa has returned to Peru to write and participate actively
in reshaping his country's political arena and social pro-
grams.   Likewise, Carlos Fuentes has returned to Mexico,
attempting to turn his intellectual-dandy status into a viable
politique that will enhance the growth of Mexico's lower and
middle classes and ensure equality of opportunity.   All of
the ten writers discussed in this book are still fantastically
popular among American literati.   Even Lezama Lima's
posthumous publication Oppiano Licario is awaiting translation into English by those who want to analyze this supposed
sequel in terms of its neo-baroque style, so successfully
utilized in its forerunner, Paradiso. [1]   Carpentier is working
assiduously on his historical tracts documenting the Castro
revolution, although very little interest has been shown here
by publishers for translation rights.   Sarduy's latest novel,
Maitreya, is a possible translator's choice for future publication, if Sarduy's hermetic style and baroque writings do
not lead him into obscurity.   Cabrera Infante continues writing film criticism and screenplays while working on other
fictional pursuits.   He recently wrote the screenplay for an
American film, Vanishing Point, which was distributed and
produced by Twentieth Century-Fox but failed dismally at
the box office.   Another new Fuentes novel and a Cortázar
short-story collection or miscellany are certain to appear on
the American publishing scene.   Even an earlier collection
of short stories by Gabriel García Márquez, The Evil Hour,
translated by Gregory Rabassa, was published in English
translation in 1980.   Gregory Kolovakos completed his excellent translation of Vargas Llosa's early novella Los
cachorros (The Cubs and Other Stories), an older collection
of the author's Peruvian tales, and Helen Lane will be
translating the new Manuel Puig novel already banned in
Argentina, Pubis angélical (Angel Hair).   Alfred E. Knopf
was planning to bring out José Donoso's latest novel, Country House, in 1980.   Certainly, the Latin American narrative is alive and well, and the ten writers discussed here
continue to be internationally and outstandingly successful.
But what has the literary "boom" spawned in terms of interest in other writers who are now coming into English translation?

     The Latin American narrative's growth in status has
led to a resurgence of interest in and a proliferation of new
and better translations of writers who have been labeled
"precursors" to the "boom" movement or have occupied
positions on the sidelines, awaiting their turn for interna-

tional recognition.   If this author were to include one other
Latin American novelist for close scrutiny in an individual
chapter, he would have added the Uruguayan Juan Carlos
Onetti.   Onetti's A Brief Life (1950), a forerunner of the
"new" Latin American narrative, was just translated in 1978.
A few years earlier, in 1968, The Shipyard (1961) reached
the United States, another brilliant Onetti novel.   Since his
role as a precursor of the "boom" novelists is so important,
let us briefly examine his life and work.

Onetti is another self-exiled writer, presently living
in Madrid because of an unjust pronouncement by military
authorities over the award of a literary prize to a story
judged "pornographic" in January 1974.   Although released
the following May, because of his participation in the event
as well as failing health, he resigned the directorship of
Uruguay's Municipal Libraries and left for Europe, where he
has remained since 1975.

Born in Montevideo on July 1, 1909, Onetti had the
advantages of the capital, the River Plate, and Buenos Aires
cultures.   He began writing in his early twenties, first as a
newspaperman, then as a short-story writer, then as a novelist.   Although he is known for many novels abroad, only
A Brief Life and The Shipyard have appeared in the United
States in translation, although The Corpse Collectors (1964)
ought to be translated in the near future.

It was indeed the "boom" of the 1960s that brought
Onetti to international attention.   In 1962 he won Uruguay's
National Prize for Literature and attended his first P. E. N.
Conference in the United States.   With the 1968 translation
of The Shipyard into English, Onetti received his long-
deserved recognition.   The reasons are fairly clear.   Onetti
is interested in the use of spoken language in his works and
readily paved the way for Cabrera Infante's Three Trapped
Tigers, Puig's Heartbreak Tango and Betrayed by Rita Hayworth, and Sarduy's Cobra.   Even these innovations of language seen in his earliest short stories are "rehearsals" for
the novels written especially by Manuel Puig.   In the words
of Djelal Kadir, "Puig's aesthetics are a culmination of a
project begun by Juan Carlos Onetti."[2]   Onetti, known for
his love of Faulknerian narrative, was the first to explore
the possibilities of a constantly shifting narrative point of
view, paving the way for Cortázar, Fuentes, Vargas Llosa,
and Puig.   Onetti is also a great mythopoeist, a creator of
myths; his books are precursors of works of mythification

like Lezama Lima's Paradiso and Carlos Fuentes's Where
the Air Is Clear and Terra Nostra. Another fascinating aspect of Onetti's work is his gift for creating fables, giving
a totality of cosmic proportions to the environments of his
novels. TTT, by Cabrera, Vargas Llosa's The Green House,
and Guimarães Rosa's The Devil to Pay in the Backlands support Onetti's tendencies toward fabulation. Finally, Onetti
approaches the level of allegory, as brought to perfection in
the Macondo setting of García Márquez's One Hundred Years
of Solitude and some of his short-story collections. Djelal
Kadir, in his excellent book on Onetti, has examined the
author's life and novels in depth. He seizes upon these four
principal points to corroborate Onetti's great role as precursor and is responsible for restoring Onetti's position of
prime importance among today's Latin American creative and
exiled novelists, whose works have been translated some
twenty years later than they should have been. [3]

Likewise, the Peruvian José Arguedas's masterpiece
Deep Rivers[4] (1958) and his compatriot Manuel Scorza's
Drums for Rancas (1970) both appeared here in 1978, indi-
cating an eight-to-ten year delay between conception and
translation. The Argentine Ernesto Sábato's early novella
The Outsider was published here in 1950, his Abbadon, The
Exterminating Angel in 1974, and his On Heros and Tombs,
currently being translated by Helen Lane for David Godine,
Publishers, was anxiously awaited in 1980. Although the
Mexican Gustavo Sainz's earlier novel Gazapo (1965) reached
American readers in 1968, one wonders what happened to
the translation of his latest novel The Princess of the Iron
Palace (1974). And what became of the Paraguayan Augusto
Roa Bastos's other novels since the publication of Son of
Man in 1961 and its English translation in 1965?

As the fallout from the "boom" in the Latin American
narrative continues to settle, a younger generation of writers
is waiting in the wings. There are a host of new Cuban
writers: Carlos Montaner's Perromundo (A Dog's World)
should be coming into English translation shortly, as well as
Matías Montés Huidobro's Exiled to the Fire, both better-
than-average, authentic examples of the anti-Castro narrative by exiles. The Colombian Gustavo Alvárez Gardeáza-
bal's The Puppeteer, a difficult surrealist work, cries out
for an American audience, as do the novels of the Argentine
Gudiño Keefer, Chile's Antonio Skármeta, Mexico's Salvador
Elizondo and José Agustín, Cuba's Reinaldo Arenas (his
Hallucinations was translated here in 1968), and Peru's

Alfredo Bryce Echínque.   Let us also keep a watchful eye
for a new Salvador Garmendia novel from Mexico like Ash
Wednesday (1964) or The Bad Life (1968) or the Cuban Ed-
mundo Desnoes's successor to Inconsolable Memories (1965)--
which was made into a memorable film by Tomas Alea--or
the Argentine Nestor Sánchez's Siberia Blues (1967) or some
of the older works by established writers in new editions,
such as the Mexican Juan Rulfo's Pedro Paramo (1970) or
José Arreola's 1963 novel The Fair (which appeared here in
1977) or Agustín Yáñez's pace-setting novel At the Edge of
the Storm (1947), which appeared here in paperback in 1963,
although his Prodigal Earth (1966) has not been translated as
yet.

There are still some literary giants who have not yet
come into translation, let alone received the recognition they
deserve: the Argentine Leopoldo Marechal's Adam Buenos
Aires (1948) and Macedonio Fernández's satirical Adriana
Buenos Aires, or his A Novel That Begins or Museum of
the Novel of Eterna.   Also, novelists like the Mexican Fernando del Paso, the Argentine Daniel Moyano, and the Argentine Mario Satz are hardly known at all in the United
States, much less in Spanish than in English.   Poet-novelist
Mario Satz's first novel, Sun (1976), appeared here in
1980 translated by Helen Lane for Doubleday, with translations of his subsequent novels, Moon (1977) and Earth (1977),
hopefully to follow. 5

An entire chapter or book could also be devoted to
the new Brazilian novel as well.   We have already seen
Clarice Lispector's Apple in the Dark and Family Ties
please American readers, as well as Graciliano Ramos's
short-story collection Barren Lives.   The latter's 1934
novel São Bernardo was just published in English here in
1978.   But what of the new translation of João Guimãraes
Rosa's The Devil to Pay in the Backlands (his short-story
collection Third Bank of the River has been popular here
for several years) or Nélida Piñón's feminist novels?   Besides the usual Jorge Amado, from Gabriela, Clove and
Cinnamon to Doña Flor and Her Two Husbands, novels that
appear with regularity, very few critics have treated themselves to the well-written novel Sergeant Getúlio, by João
Ubaldo Riberio, which appeared here in 1979.

Another chapter that could be added to this book
would be on Latin American women writers and their contributions to the contemporary literary scene. 6   Only

recently Argentine Luisa Valenzuela's collections of novellas
and short stories have come into English translation--Strange
Things Happen Here (1979), for example--but no one hears of
any other formidable female Latin American writers north of
the Río Grande.   An exception is Victoria Ocampo, chiefly
because of Doris Meyer's excellent biography published in
1979 by George Brazillier, which also contains some of
Ocampo's writings.   Ocampo was the founder of the well-
known literary magazine Sur and the great compatriot of
Jorge Luis Borges and Adolfo Bioy-Casares, whose works
have been translated in the United States since the mid-1930s
up to the present.   The same holds true for the gifted Nobel
Prize-winner Miguel Angel Asturias of Guatemala, whose
1949 novel Men of Maize appeared here in 1975, some twenty-
six years later.

As younger, major Latin American writers are sur-
facing because of their own talent and aided by the impetus
of the "boom," better translators in the fields of Spanish,
Portuguese, and Latin American literature are also coming
to the fore.   American literary reviewers are no longer
singularly interested just in the fiction, its aesthetic values
and its authors' biographies, but are making critical judg-
ments of translators and their art as well.   There is certainly a very talented group of American critics and translators, who with their unparalleled efforts have provided the
Latin American narrative with its long-overdue rebirth in
this century.

"Latin Americans have, at long last," writes Monegal, "become true contemporaries, if not in fact, the van-
guard of all mankind."7   Over the past twenty years the
Latin American narrative has received the widest exposure
it has ever known here and abroad.   Robert G. Mead writes:

> Now that the "boom" has subsided and left behind
> what we all hope will be a permanent interest in
> Latin American writing, the time has come ... for
> authors, critics, publishers and readers all over
> the Hemisphere to utilize this interest in the larger
> and longer term enterprise of making possible the
> reading and critical evaluation of the great books
> of the past in all genres in Latin America, so that
> all of us, North and South Americans, can gain a
> truer and fuller understanding of the New World's
> literary and cultural heritage in the three great
> languages of the Hemisphere. 8

May the 1980s also accord the Latin American narrative its well-earned national and international stature. [9]

CHAPTER NOTES

Chapter One

1. Emir Rodríguez Monegal corroborates Carpentier's French ancestry and says the latter speaks Spanish with a distinctly gallic r, as noted in Monegal's The Borzoi Anthology of Latin American Literature, Vol. II (New York: Knopf, 1977), p. 517.
2. Ibid., p. 518.
3. Idem.
4. Lecture notes from a class given at the New School of Social Research by Professor Monegal in the Fall 1978 semester.
5. Enrique Anderson-Imbert, Spanish-American Literature: A History, Vol. II (Detroit: Wayne State University Press, 1969), p. 635.
6. Gordon Brotherston, The Emergence of the Latin American Novel (Cambridge, England: Cambridge University Press, 1977), p. 48.
7. Jean Franco, An Introduction to Spanish-American Literature (Cambridge, England: Cambridge University Press, 1969), pp. 317-318.
8. Ibid., p. 319.
9. Anderson-Imbert, p. 636.
10. Franco, p. 239.
11. Luis Harss, Into the Mainstream (New York: Harper, 1967), p. 64.
12. Ibid., p. 66.
13. John S. Brushwood, The Spanish American Novel (Austin: University of Texas Press, 1975), p. 222.
14. David W. Foster and Virginia R. Foster, Modern Latin American Literature, Vol. I (New York: Ungar, 1975), p. 218.

15.   Ibid., p. 225.
16.   Ibid., p. 222.
17.   Foster, pp. 218-219.
18.   Ibid., p. 221.
19.   Kessel Schwartz, A New History of Spanish American Fiction, Vol. II (Coral Gables: University of Miami Press, 1971), p. 204.
20.   Idem.
21.   Alexander Coleman, "Book Review of Reasons of State," New York Times Book Review (May 2, 1976), p. 51.
22.   Idem.

Chapter Two

1.   David W. Foster, A Dictionary of Contemporary Latin American Authors (Tempe, Arizona: Arizona University Press, 1975), p. 30.
2.   Philip Ward, The Oxford Companion to Spanish Literature (England: Oxford University Press, 1978), p. 488.
3.   Emir Rodríguez Monegal, The Borzoi Anthology of Latin American Literature, Vol. II (New York: Knopf, 1977), p. 718.
4.   Gordon Brotherston, The Emergence of the Latin American Novel (Cambridge, England: Cambridge University Press, 1977), p. 94.
5.   Dust jacket for Julio Cortázar, A Manual for Manuel (New York: Pantheon, 1978).
6.   Idem.
7.   John Incledon, "Cortázar's 'Silent Performance' in A Manual for Manuel," Latin American Section, M.L.A. Convention, New York, Dec. 27, 1977.
8.   Idem.
9.   Idem.
10.   Brotherston, p. 94.
11.   John Sturrock, "Book Review of A Manual for Manuel," New York Times Book Review (Feb. 19, 1978), pp. 30-32.
12.   John Leonard, "Books of the Times: A Manual for Manuel," New York Times (Nov. 13, 1978), p. 28.
13.   Idem.
14.   Frank MacShane, "Visit from Julio Cortázar," New York Times Book Review (Feb. 12, 1978), p. 3.
15.   Idem.
16.   Idem.
17.   Idem.
18.   Incledon lecture.

19. Jaime Alazraki and Ivar Ivask, eds., The Final Island (Norman: University of Oklahoma Press, 1978), p. 17.
20. Idem.
21. Ibid., p. 62.
22. Ibid., p. 164.
23. Evelyn Picon Garfield, Julio Cortázar (New York: Ungar, 1975), p. 132.
24. Ibid., p. 133.
25. Ibid., p. 139.
26. Julio Cortázar, A Manual for Manuel, dust jacket.

Chapter Three

1. Julio Cortázar, "An Ever-Present Beacon," Review '76 (Fall 1976), p. 30.
2. Emir Rodríguez Monegal, The Borzoi Anthology of Latin American Literature, Vol. II (New York: Knopf, 1977), p. 628.
3. E. Anderson-Imbert, Spanish American Literature: A History, Vol. II (Detroit: Wayne State University Press, 1969), p. 587.
4. Cortázar, p. 30.
5. Peter Winn, "Literary Letter from Cuba," New York Times Book Review (June 3, 1979), pp. 13, 36-39.
6. Ibid., p. 37.
7. Idem.
8. Idem.
9. David W. Foster, Modern Latin American Literature, Vol. I (New York: Ungar, 1975), p. 482.   J. M. Cohen review cited.
10. J. Lezama Lima, Paradiso (New York: Farrar, Straus and Giroux, 1974), dust jacket.
11. Winn, p. 38.
12. Edmund White, "Review of Paradiso," New York Times Book Review (Apr. 21, 1974), p. 27.
13. Idem.
14. John Alfred Avant, "Review of Paradiso," New Republic (June 15, 1974), p. 27.
15. Julio Cortázar, "An Approach to Lezama Lima," Review '74 (Fall 1974), p. 21.
16. Klaus Müller-Bergh, "José Lezama Lima and Paradiso," Books Abroad (Winter 1970), p. 38.
17. Raymond D. Souza, Major Cuban Novelists (Columbia: University of Missouri Press, 1976), p. 56.
18. Ibid., p. 57.
19. Ibid., p. 61.

20. Ibid., p. 76.
21. Idem.
22. Ibid., p. 77.
23. Idem.
24. Arthur J. Sabatini, "On Reading Paradiso," Latin American Section, M. L. A. Conference, New York, Dec. 27, 1977.
25. David W. Foster, A Dictionary of Contemporary Latin American Authors (Tempe: Arizona State University Press, 1975), p. 60.
26. Monegal, p. 629.
27. Kessel Schwartz, The New History of Spanish American Fiction, Vol. II (Coral Gables: University of Miami Press, 1971), p. 206.
28. David Gallagher, "Review of Paradiso," New York Review of Books, Vol. 10, No. 10 (May 23, 1968).
29. Mario Vargas Llosa, "Attempting the Impossible," Review '74 (Fall 1974), p. 29.
30. Idem.
31. Julio Ortega, "Language as Hero," Review '74 (Fall 1974), p. 39.
32. J. M. Alonso, "A Sentimental Realism," Review '74 (Fall 1974), p. 46.
33. Ibid., p. 47.

Chapter Four

1. Mario Vargas Llosa, "From Aracataca to Macondo," Review '70 (1970), p. 129.
2. Idem.
3. It is interesting to note that famed critic Guillermo de la Torre rejected Leaf Storm for publication by Editorial Losada and urged García Márquez to try another line of work.
4. Mario Vargas Llosa, "Chronology," Books Abroad, Vol. 47, No. 3 (1973), p. 504.
5. William Kennedy, "Review of The Autumn of the Patriarch," New York Times (Oct. 31, 1976), p. 1.
6. Idem.
7. Most of the biographical material in this chapter has been compiled from information available in the following: George R. McMurray, Gabriel García Márquez (New York: Ungar, 1977), pp. viii-x); Mario Vargas Llosa, Gabriel García Márquez: History of a Deicide (Barcelona: Seix Barral, 1971), pp. 13-84; World Authors: 1950-1970, edited by John Wakeman (New York:

Wilson, 1975), pp. 525-527; and Books Abroad, Vol. 47, No. 3 (Summer 1973), pp. 501-504.

8. See Frank McShane, "Márquez Himself," New York Times Book Review (July 16, 1978), pp. 3, 23.

9. Bradley Shaw, Latin American Literature in English Translation: 1976-1978, Addendum (New York: NYU Press, 1979), p. 12.

10. Gregory Rabassa, "Beyond Magic Realism: Thoughts on the Art of García Márquez," Books Abroad, Vol. 47, No. 3 (1973), p. 450.

11. Kennedy, p. 1.

12. Stephen Koch, "Review of The Autumn of the Patriarch," Saturday Review (Dec. 11, 1976), p. 68.

13. R. Z. Sheppard, "Review of The Autumn of the Patriarch," Time (Nov. 1, 1976), p. 87.

14. Alastair Reid, "Basilisk's Eggs," New Yorker (Nov. 8, 1976), pp. 175-204.

15. Kennedy, p. 1.

16. Christopher Lehmann-Haupt, "A Fever in the Quills," New York Times (Nov. 3, 1976), p. 37.

17. George R. McMurray, Gabriel García Márquez (New York: Ungar, 1977), pp. 153-154.

18. Idem.

19. Kennedy, p. 16.

20. Koch, p. 68.

21. Kennedy, p. 16.

22. Reid, p. 207.

23. Kessel Schwartz, A New History of Spanish American Literature, Vol. II (Coral Gables: University of Miami Press, 1971), p. 141.

24. Koch, p. 68.

25. Walter Clemons, "Book Review," Newsweek (Nov. 7, 1976). No page listed.

26. Kennedy, p. 1.

27. McMurray, p. 156.

28. Emir Rodríguez Monegal, The Borzoi Anthology of Latin American Literature, Volume II (New York: Knopf, 1977), pp. 886-887.

29. Paul West, "Review of The Autumn of the Patriarch," Review '76 (Fall 1976), p. 58.

30. Idem.

31. Idem.

32. McMurray, p. 156.

33. New York Times Book Review (Dec. 5, 1976), p. 103.

34. McMurray, p. 156.

Chapter Five

1. The biographical material about Mario Vargas Llosa is based for the most part upon the chronologies in two principal sources: Review '75 No. 14 (Spring 1975), pp. 6-11, and Texas Studies in Literature and Language, Vol. X, No. 4 (Winter 1977), pp. 560-561.
2. José Miguel Oviedo, "Interview with Mario Vargas Llosa," as reported by Wolfgang A. Luchtig in Hispania Vol. 58, No. 1 (March 1975), pp. 216-217.
3. Idem.
4. William L. Siemens, "Apollo's Metamorphosis in Pantaleón y las visitadoras," Texas Studies in Literature and Language Vol. XIX, No. 4 (Winter 1977), p. 483.
5. Robert Brody, "Capt. Pantoja and the Special Service: A Review" Unpublished paper, Latin American Section, Montclair State College, New Jersey, March 16, 1978, p. 4.
6. "Peruvian Novelist Turns Film Maker and Tangles with the Army," New York Times, Nov. 22, 1977, p. 38.
7. Siemens, p. 481.
8. Ronald Christ, "Talk with Vargas Llosa," New York Times Book Review (April 9, 1978), pp. 3, 38.
9. Barbara Probst Solomon, "Review of Capt. Pantoja and the Special Service," New York Times (April 9, 1978), p. 11.
10. Idem.
11. Christ, p. 38.
12. Idem.
13. Mario Vargas Llosa, "Literature Is Fire," translated by Maureen Ahern de Maurer, as quoted in H. Carpenter and J. Brof, Doors and Mirrors (New York: Viking, 1972), pp. 432-437.
14. Christ, p. 38.
15. Idem.

Chapter Six

1. Most of the biographical material available on Cabrera Infante comes from his own account in the form of a "Chronology," which he authored originally in Spanish, "written in the style of Laurence Sterne"; it appeared translated in Review '72 No. 4-5: Focus on Cabrera Infante (1972), pp. 5-9.
2. David W. Foster, Dictionary of Latin American Authors,

(Tempe: University of Arizona Press, 1975), p. 21.
3. Kessel Schwartz, A New History of Spanish American
    Fiction, Vol. II (Coral Gables: University of Miami
    Press, 1971), p. 210.
4. David W. Foster, Modern Latin American Authors,
    Vol. I (New York: Ungar, 1975), p. 201.
5. Raymond D. Souza, Major Cuban Novelists (Columbia,
    Missouri: University of Missouri Press, 1976), p. 84.
6. Foster, Modern Latin American Authors, p. 202.
7. G. Cabrera Infante, View of Dawn in the Tropics,
    translated by Suzanne Jill Levine (New York: Harper,
    1978), dust jacket.
8. Julio Hernández-Miyares, "Cabrera Infante: A Tiger
    in the Tropics," Unpublished paper, February 15, 1977.
9. Michael Robertson, "A Cuban Ballet Star Who Cuts
    Sugar Cane," New York Times (July 15, 1979),
    pp. 19, 24.

Chapter Seven

1. Most of the biographical information on Carlos Fuentes
    comes from World Authors 1950-1970, edited by John
    Wakeman (New York: Wilson, 1975), pp. 509-511.
2. Idem.
3. Emir Rodríguez Monegal, The Borzoi Anthology of Latin
    American Literature, Vol. II (New York: Knopf, 1977),
    p. 874.
4. Juan Goytisolo, "Our New World," Review '76 (1976),
    pp. 4-24.
5. The majority of critical adjectives attributed to Terra
    Nostra come from these reviews of the novel: Robert
    Coover, New York Times (Nov. 7, 1976), pp. 3, 48;
    Robert Maurer, Saturday Review (Nov. 1, 1976), p. 47;
    and Peter S. Prescott, Newsweek (Nov. 15, 1976),
    p. 44.
6. Joseph Sommers, After the Storm (Albuquerque: Uni-
    versity of New Mexico Press, 1968), p. 96.
7. John Leonard, "Review of The Hydra Head," quoted on
    dust jacket.
8. Anthony Burgess, "Review of The Hydra Head," New
    York Times (Jan. 7, 1979), p. 1.

Chapter Eight

1. Interview with Manuel Puig at the New School for Social

Research, New York City, April 15, 1976.

2. Most of this biographical information is based upon Manuel Puig's own words, "Growing Up in the Movies: A Chronology," Review '72 No. 4-5 (1972), pp. 49-51.
3. Idem.
4. Interview notes.
5. Idem.
6. Puig, Review '72, p. 51.
7. Alexander Coleman, "Review of Betrayed by Rita Hayworth," New York Times (Sept. 26, 1971), p. 3.
8. Interview notes.
9. Philip Ward, ed., The Oxford Companion to Spanish Literature (Oxford: Oxford University Press, 1978), p. 477.
10. Emir Rodríguez Monegal, The Borzoi Anthology of Latin American Literature, Vol. II (New York: Knopf, 1977), p. 927.
11. Idem.
12. Emir Rodríguez Monegal, "A Literary Myth Exploded," Review '72 No. 4-5 (1972), p. 64.
13. For this particular biographical aspect of Puig's life, see John S. Brushwood, The Spanish American Novel (Austin: University of Texas Press, 1975), p. 307.
14. Interview notes.
15. Monegal, Borzoi Anthology, p. 928.
16. Idem.
17. Interview notes.
18. Idem.
19. For an interesting discussion of camp, read Susan Sontag's "Notes on Camp" in her collection of essays, Against Interpretation (New York: Delta, 1967, 1972), pp. 275-292.
20. Manuel Puig, Heartbreak Tango (New York: Dutton, 1973), dust jacket.
21. Monegal, Borzoi Anthology, p. 928.
22. Idem.
23. Manuel Puig, Kiss of the Spiderwoman (New York: Knopf, 1979), dust jacket.
24. Peter S. Prescott, "Movie Dreams in Argentina," Newsweek (May 7, 1979), pp. 92-93.
25. Christopher Lehmann-Haupt, "Review of Kiss of the Spiderwoman," New York Times (April 23, 1979), p. 17.
26. Robert Aller, "Review of The Buenos Aires Affair," New York Times (April 23, 1979), p. 17.
27. Idem.
28. Lehmann-Haupt, p. 17.

29. Monegal, Borzoi Anthology, p. 926.
30. Brushwood, p. 307.
31. Alfred J. MacAdam, "Things as They Are," in Modern Latin American Narratives (Chicago: University of Chicago Press, 1977), p. 99.
32. Brushwood, p. 308.
33. MacAdam, p. 100.
34. Ronald Christ, "Fact or Fiction," Review '73 (1973), p. 54.
35. David W. Foster, Currents in the Contemporary Argentine Novel (Columbia: University of Missouri Press, 1975), p. 148.
36. D. P. Gallagher, Modern Latin American Literature (New York: Oxford University Press, 1973), pp. 186-187.
37. Ibid., p. 188.

Chapter Nine

1. Jerome Charnyn, "Review of Cobra," New York Times (May 9, 1975), p. 3.
2. Idem.
3. Severy Sarduy, "Chronology," Review '72 No. 6 (1972), p. 24.
4. Idem.
5. Ibid., p. 26.
6. John Brushwood, The Spanish American Novel (Austin: University of Texas Press, 1976), p. 300.
7. Emir Rodríguez Monegal, The Borzoi Anthology of Latin American Literature, Vol. II (New York: Knopf, 1977), p. 951.
8. Idem.
9. Much of the biographical information in the preceding paragraphs is drawn from Severo Sarduy's own "Chronicle," Review '72 No. 6 (1972), pp. 24-27.
10. It is in the lotus image that Cobra becomes recognizable as a continuation of Part One of From Cuba with a Song, metamorphized into her (his) new fictional presence.
11. Jean-Michel Fossey, "From Boom to Big-Bang," Review '74 No. 13 (1974), p. 12.
12. Suzanne Jill Levine, "Preface," in S. Sarduy's Cobra (New York: Dutton, 1975), p. x.
13. Ibid., p. xi.
14. Suzanne Jill Levine, "Translated Selection from Cobra," Review '72 No. 6 (1972), p. 37, footnote.

15.   Charnyn, p. 3.
16.   Monegal, p. 951.
17.   Robert M. Adams, "Shrill Chill," Review '74 No. 13
       (1974), p. 24.
18.   Ibid., p. 25.
19.   Levine, "Preface," p. x.
20.   Charnyn, p. 3.

Chapter Ten

1.   See Severo Sarduy, "Writing/Transvestism," Review
      '73 No. 9 (1973), pp. 31-33, on Donoso's aesthetics
      and "Heartbreak Tango: Parody and Grafting," Sur
      No. 34 (Aug.-Dec. 1969), pp. 71-77, and "Notes on
      notes on notes...," Revista Iberoamericana No. 76-77
      (1971), pp. 555-567 for two discussions of Manuel
      Puig's works.
2.   Unidentified critical responses, Review '73 No. 9
      (1973), p. 11.
3.   Philip Ward, ed., The Oxford Companion to Spanish
      Literature (Oxford: Oxford University Press, 1978),
      p. 171.
4.   Emir Rodríguez Monegal, The Borzoi Anthology of Latin
      American Literature, Vol. II (New York: Knopf, 1977),
      p. 865.
5.   For a discussion of influences on Donoso's writing as
      well as the phenomenon known as the "boom," see his
      essay The Boom in Spanish American Literature: A
      Personal History, translated by Gregory Kolovakos
      (New York: Columbia University Press, 1977).
6.   Paul West, "The Sanskrit Everyone Knows," Review '77
      No. 20 (1977), p. 67.
7.   Anatole Broyard, "The Exile Who Lost His Tongue,"
      New York Times (June 26, 1977), p. 14.
8.   Most of the biographical information in this section
      comes from the author's own account in his "Chronolo-
      gy," Review '73 No. 9 (1973), pp. 12-19, and George
      R. McMurray, José Donoso (Boston: Twayne Pubs.,
      1979), pp. 11-13.
9.   José Donoso, "Chronology," p. 15.
10.   Idem.
11.   Monegal, p. 864.
12.   Donoso, "Chronology," p. 18.
13.   Ibid., p. 19.
14.   Donoso, The Boom in Spanish American Literature,
      p. 115.

15. McMurray, José Donoso (Boston: Twayne Pubs.,
     1979), pp. 136-137.
16. Monegal, p. 864.
17. Broyard, p. 14.
18. McMurray, p. 146.
19. Broyard, p. 14.
20. R. Z. Sheppard, "Review: Sacred Families," Time
     Vol. 109 (June 27, 1979), p. 68.
21. McMurray, pp. 146-147.
22. José Donoso, Sacred Families (New York: Knopf,
     1977), dust jacket.
23. R. Z. Sheppard, p. 68.
24. Kessel Schwartz, A New History of Spanish American
     Literature, Vol. II (Coral Gables: University of Miami
     Press, 1971), p. 159.
25. Emir Rodríguez Monegal, "José Donoso," Mundo Nuevo
     No. 12 (July 1967), pp. 77, 85.

Conclusion

1. As this book was going to press, Lezama Lima's
    sequel to Paradiso, Oppiano Licario, was published in
    Mexico by Ed. Era in a Clave Paperback edition with
    a 1978 copyright.   It has yet to appear here in Eng-
    lish translation.
2. Djelal Kadir, Juan Carlos Onetti (Boston: Twayne
    Pubs., 1977), p. 146.
3. See the footnote above as well as Review '75 No. 16
    (Winter 1975), pp. 4-33:   Focus on Onetti, celebrating
    the publication of A Brief Life in English.
4. The Peruvian José Arguedas's masterpiece was pub-
    lished here in 1978.   The author committed suicide in
    May of 1969 and was unable to enjoy his posthumous
    international success, as his compatriot Mario Vargas
    Llosa noted in the Afterword he wrote especially for
    the American translation in the University of Texas
    Press edition.
5. Review '79 No. 24 (1979) just published a "Focus on
    Mario Satz," as well as a sadly overdue and posthum-
    ous "focus" on the great Brazilian novelist Clarice
    Lispector.
6. Scarecrow Press has brought out a volume on this sub-
    ject in 1980 entitled Women Novelists in Spain and
    Spanish America by Lucía Fox-Lockert, dealing with
    twenty-two female novelists from a sociological and
    feminist viewpoint.

7. Emir Rodríguez Monegal, The Borzoi Anthology of Latin American Literature, Vol. II (New York: Knopf, 1977), Preface, p. xiv.
8. Robert G. Mead, "After the Boom," Americas Vol. 30, No. 4 (April 4, 1978), p. 8.
9. For further overviews of Latin American literature, consult these four articles, all written by the prolific critic E. R. Monegal: "The New Latin American Literature in the U. S. A.," Review '68 No. 1 (1968), pp. 3-13; "Introduction and Prefaces," Borzoi Anthology; "Latin American Literature," in World Literature Since 1945 (New York: Ungar, 1973), pp. 416-448; "A Revolutionary Writing," Mundus Atrium Vol. 3, No. 3 (Summer 1970), pp. 6-11.

SELECTED BIBLIOGRAPHY

The following is intended as a selective guide to further
reading. It comprises the principal texts described in the
book, some useful anthologies and editions of complete
works, translations into English, and important works of
criticism.

Introduction

Anderson-Imbert, Enrique. Spanish-American Literature:
   A History. 2 vols. Detroit: Wayne State University
   Press, 1969.
Brotherston, Gordon. The Emergence of the Latin American
   Novel. Cambridge, England: Cambridge University Press,
   1977.
Brushwood, John S. The Spanish American Novel. Austin:
   University of Texas Press, 1975.
Donoso, José. The Boom in Spanish American Literature:
   A Personal History. New York: Columbia University
   Press, 1977.
Foster, David W. The Twentieth Century Spanish-American
   Novel: A Bibliographic Guide. Metuchen, N.J.: Scare-
   crow, 1975.
Foster, David W., and Virginia R. Foster. Modern Latin
   American Literature. 2 vols. New York: Ungar, 1975.
   Criticism.
Franco, Jean. An Introduction to Spanish-American Litera-
   ture. Cambridge, England: Cambridge University Press,
   1969.
_____. The Modern Culture of Latin America: Society
   and the Artist. New York: Praeger, 1967.
Gallagher, D. P. Modern Latin American Literature. New
   York: Oxford University Press, 1973.

Monegal, Emir Rodríguez. The Borzoi Anthology of Latin
    American Literature. 2 vols. New York: Knopf, 1977.
Schwartz, Kessel. A New History of Spanish American Fic-
    tion. 2 vols. Miami: University of Miami Press, 1971.
Shaw, Bradley A. Latin American Literature in English
    Translation: An Annotated Bibliography. New York:
    New York University Press, 1976.

Chapter One - Alejo Carpentier

Translations

Carpentier, Alejo. The Lost Steps. Tr. Harriet de Onís.
    New York: Knopf, 1956.
    _____. The Kingdom of This World. Tr. Harriet de
    Onís. New York: Knopf, 1957.
    _____. "Manhunt." Tr. Harriet de Onís. Noonday, 2
    (1959), 109-180.
    _____. Explosion in a Cathedral. Tr. John Sturrock.
    London: Gollancz, 1963.
    _____. War of Time. Tr. Frances Partridge. New
    York: Knopf, 1970.
    _____. Reasons of State. Tr. Frances Partridge. New
    York: Knopf, 1976.

Selected Studies on Carpentier

Books

González-Echeverría, Roberto. Alejo Carpentier: The Pil-
    grim at Home. Ithaca, N. Y.: Cornell University Press,
    1977.
Skinner, Eugene. Archetypal Patterns in Four Novels of
    Alejo Carpentier. Kansas University, 1970. Doctoral
    Dissertation.

Articles

Adams, Ralston P. "The Search for the Indigenous: An
    Evolution of the Literary Vision of Alejo Carpentier and
    Miguel Angel Asturias," in Beck, M., Davis, L., Her-
    nández, J., and Keller, G., eds., The Analysis of
    Hispanic Texts: Current Trends in Methodology. Jamaica,
    N. Y.: Bilingual Press, York College, 1976.
Flores, Angel. "Magical Realism in Spanish American Fic-
    tion." Hispania 38 (1955), 187-192.

González-Echeverría, Roberto.   "The Parting of the Waters."
    Diacritics Vol. 4 (1974), pp. 8-17.
Jiménez-Fajardo, Salvador.   "The Redeeming Quest: Pat-
    terns of Unification in Carpentier, Fuentes and Cortázar."
    Revista de estudios hispánicos (University of Alabama)
    Vol. 11 (1977), pp. 91-117.
Kilmer-Tchalekion, Mary A.   "Ambiguities in El siglo de
    las luces (Explosion in a Cathedral)."   Latin American
    Literary Review Vol. 8 (1976), pp. 47-55.
Müller-Bergh, Klaus.   "Talking to Carpentier."   Review
    Vol. 18 (1976), pp. 20-24.   (Tr. Andrée Conrad.)
Pérez-Reilly, Elizabeth Kranz.   "Lo real maravilloso in the
    Prose Fiction of Alejo Carpentier: A Critical Study."
    Dissertation Abstracts International Vol. 36 (1976),
    pp. 4532A-4533A.

Chapter Two - Julio Cortázar

Translations

Cortázar, Julio.   The Winners.   Tr. Elaine Kerrigan.   New
    York: Pantheon, 1965.
_____.   Hopscotch.   Tr. Gregory Rabassa.   New York:
    Pantheon, 1966.
_____.   End of the Game and Other Stories.   Tr. Paul
    Blackburn.   New York: Pantheon, 1967.
_____.   Cronopios and Famas.   Tr. Paul Blackburn.
    New York: Pantheon, 1969.
_____.   62:   A Model Kit.   Tr. Gregory Rabassa.   New
    York: Pantheon, 1966.
_____.   All Fires the Fire and Other Stories.   Tr.
    Suzanne Jill Levine.   New York: Pantheon, 1973.
_____.   A Manual for Manuel.   Tr. Gregory Rabassa.
    New York: Pantheon, 1978.

Selected Studies on Cortázar

Books

Alazraki, Jaime, and Ivan Ivask.   The Final Island.   Nor-
    man: University of Oklahoma Press, 1978.
Garfield, Evelyn Picon.   Julio Cortázar.   New York:
    Ungar, 1975.

Articles

Center for Inter-American Relations.   Review '72: Focus
on Julio Cortázar.   New York: Center for Inter-Am.
Relations, 1972.
Safir, Margery A.   "An Erotics of Liberation: Notes on
Trangressive Behavior in Hopscotch and A Manual for
Manuel."   Books Abroad Vol. 50, No. 3 (Summer 1976),
pp. 558-570.
Valentine, Robert.   "The Artist's Quest for Freedom in
A Manual for Manuel."   Chasqui Vol. 3, No. 2 (February
1974), pp. 62-74.

Chapter Three - José Lezama Lima

Translations

Lezama Lima, José.   Paradiso.   Tr. Gregory Rabassa.
New York: Farrar, Straus and Giroux, 1974.

Selected Studies on Lezama Lima

Books

Souza, Raymond D.   Major Cuban Novelists.   Columbia:
University of Missouri Press, 1976.

Articles

Center for Inter-American Relations.   Review '74: Focus
on Paradiso.   New York: Center for Inter-Amer. Rela-
tions, 1974.
Moscoso-Góngora, Peter.   "A Proust of the Caribbean."
Nation Vol. 218 (May 11, 1974), pp. 1600-1601.
Pérez Firmat, Gustavo.   "Descent into Paradiso: A Study
of Heaven and Homosexuality."   Hispania 59 (1976),
pp. 247-257.
Persin, Margo.   "Language as Form and Content in
Paradiso."   The American Hispanist Vol. 1, No. viii
(1976), pp. 11-17.
Waller, Claudia J.   "José Lezama Lima's Paradiso: The
Theme of Light and the Resurrection."   Hispania 56
(1973), pp. 275-282.
Wood, Michael.   "José Lezama Lima's Paradiso."   New
York Review of Books Vol. 21, No. 6 (April 18, 1974),
pp. 14-16.

Chapter Four - Gabriel García Márquez

Translations

García Márquez, Gabriel.   No One Writes to the Colonel and
    Other Stories.   Tr. J. S. Bernstein.   New York: Harper,
    1968.
_____.   One Hundred Years of Solitude.   Tr. Gregory
    Rabassa.   New York: Harper, 1970.
_____.   Leaf Storm and Other Stories.   Tr. Gregory
    Rabassa.   New York: Harper, 1972.
_____.   The Autumn of the Patriarch.   Tr. Gregory
    Rabassa.   New York: Harper, 1976.
_____.   Innocent Eréndira and Other Stories.   Tr. Greg-
    ory Rabassa.   New York: Harper, 1978.

Selected Studies on García Márquez

Books

McMurray, George R.   Gabriel García Márquez.   New York:
    Ungar, 1977.

Articles

Books Abroad Vol. 47, No. 3 (Summer 1973), pp. 439-512.
Center for Inter-American Relations.   Review '70: Focus
    on García Márquez.   New York: Center for Inter-Am.
    Relations, Vol. 3, 1971, pp. 97-191.
Oberhelman, Harley D.   "Faulknerian Techniques in García
    Márquez' Portrait of a Dictator."   Unpublished paper.
    Latin American Section, Texas Technological University,
    Lubbock, Texas, Jan. 24, 1977.
_____.   "G. García Márquez and the American South."
    Chasqui Vol. 5, No. 1 (1975), pp. 29-38.
Vargas Llosa, Mario.   "G. García Márquez: From
    Aracataca to Macondo."   Review '70, pp. 129-142.

Chapter Five - Mario Vargas Llosa

Translations

Vargas Llosa, Mario.   A Time of the Hero.   Tr. Lysander
    Kemp.   New York: Grove, 1969.
_____.   The Green House.   Tr. Gregory Rabassa.   New
    York: Harper, 1968.

_____.   Conversations in the Cathedral.   Tr. Gregory
Rabassa.   New York: Harper, 1975.
_____.   Captain Pantoja and the Special Service.   Tr.
Gregory Kolovakos and Ronald Christ.   New York: Har-
per, 1978.

Selected Studies on Vargas Llosa

Books

Díez, Luis Alfonso.   Mario Vargas Llosa's Pursuit of the
Total Novel.   Cuernavaca, Mexico: Centro Intercultural
de Documentación, 1970.   [CIDOC Cuaderno, No. 2]

Articles

Center for Inter-American Relations.   Review '75:   Focus
on Mario Vargas Llosa Vol. 14 (Spring 1975), pp. 5-37.
Lernoux, Penny.   "The Latin American Disease: From the
Novels of Vargas Llosa."   Nation 22 (November 1974),
pp. 522-527.
Lewis, Martin A.   "Reading Pantaleón y las visitadoras."
Hispania 60 (1976), pp. 77-81.
McMurray, George R.   "The Novels of Mario Vargas Llosa."
Modern Language Quarterly 29 (1968), pp. 329-340.
Texas Studies in Literature and Language: Focus on Mario
Vargas Llosa Vol. XIX, No. 4 (Winter 1977), pp. 395-
564.
Tusa, Babs M.   "An Interpretation of Vargas Llosa's
Pantaleón y las visitadoras."   Revista de Estudios
Hispanicos 11 (1976), pp. 27-53.

Chapter Six - Guillermo Cabrera Infante

Translations

Cabrera Infante, Guillermo.   Three Trapped Tigers.   Tr.
Donald Gardner and Suzanne Jill Levine in collaboration
with the author.   New York: Harper, 1971.
_____.   View of Dawn in the Tropics.   Tr. Suzanne Jill
Levine.   New York: Harper, 1978.

Selected Studies on Cabrera Infante

Books

Souza, Raymond D.   Major Cuban Novelists.   Columbia:
University of Missouri Press, 1976.   pp. 80-108.

Articles

Guibert, Rita.   "The Tongue-twisted Tiger: An Interview
with Cabrera Infante."   Review '72 No. 4-5 (1972),
pp. 10-16.
_____.   "Interview with Cabrera Infante," in her Seven
Voices (New York: Knopf, 1973), pp. 338-436.
Sarris, Andrew.   "Rerunning Puig and Cabrera Infante."
Review '73 No. 9 (1973), pp. 46-48.
Souza, Raymond D.   "Language Versus Structure in the Con-
temporary Spanish American Novel."   Hispania Vol. 52
(1969), pp. 833-839.

Chapter Seven - Carlos Fuentes

Translations

Fuentes, Carlos.   Where the Air Is Clear.   Tr. Sam Hile-
man.   New York: Ivan Obolensky, 1960.
_____.   The Good Conscience.   Tr. Sam Hileman.   New
York: Ivan Obolensky, 1961.
_____.   The Death of Artemio Cruz.   Tr. Sam Hileman.
New York: Farrar, Straus and Giroux, 1964.
_____.   Aura.   Tr. Lysander Kemp.   New York: Farrar,
Straus and Giroux, 1965.
_____.   A Change of Skin.   Tr. Sam Hileman.   New
York: Farrar, Straus and Giroux, 1968.
_____.   Holy Place.   Tr. Suzanne Jill Levine, in Triple
Cross: Three Short Novels.   New York: Dutton, 1972.
_____.   Terra Nostra.   Tr. Margaret Sayers Peden.
New York: Farrar, Straus and Giroux, 1976.
_____.   The Hydra Head.   Tr. Margaret Sayers Peden.
New York: Farrar, Straus and Giroux, 1978.

Selected Studies on Carlos Fuentes

Books

Guzman, Daniel de. Carlos Fuentes. New York: Twayne
Pubs. , 1972.

Articles

Brushwood, John S. Mexico in Its Novel. Austin: Univer-
sity of Texas Press, 1966, pp. 36-41. Chapter on Carlos Fuentes.
Harss, Luis, and Barbara Dohmann. "Carlos Fuentes or
the New Heresy, " in Into the Mainstream. New York:
Harper, 1967, pp. 276-309.
Langford, Walter M. "Carlos Fuentes, 'The Very Model of
a Modern Major Novelist,' " in his The Mexican Novel
Comes of Age. Notre Dame: University of Notre Dame
Press, 1971, pp. 127-150.
Sommers, Joseph. "The Quest for Identity" and "The Field
of Choice: Carlos Fuentes, " in After the Storm. Albuquerque: University of New Mexico Press, 1968,
pp. 97-152 and 153-164.

Chapter Eight - Manuel Puig

Translations

Puig, Manuel. Betrayed by Rita Hayworth. Tr. Suzanne
Jill Levine. New York: Dutton, 1971.
_____ . Heartbreak Tango: A Serial. Tr. Suzanne Jill
Levine. New York: Dutton, 1973.
_____ . The Buenos Aires Affair: A Detective Novel.
Tr. Suzanne Jill Levine. New York: Dutton, 1976.
_____ . Kiss of the Spiderwoman. Tr. Thomas Colchie.
New York: Knopf, 1979.

Selected Studies on Manuel Puig

Articles

Cheuse, Alan. "Betrayed by a Celluloid Beauty. " Los
Angeles Times (Nov. 28, 1971), page unknown.
Christ, Ronald. "Fact and Fiction. " Review '73 No. 9
(1973), pp. 49-54.

_____. "Review: The Buenos Aires Affair." Panorama
(May 17, 1973), pp. 62-63.
_____. "An Interview with Manuel Puig." Partisan Re-
view Vol. 44 (1977), pp. 52-61.
Foster, David W. "Manuel Puig and the Uses of Nostalgia."
Latin American Literary Review Vol. I, No. 1 (1972),
pp. 79-81.
Gallagher, D. P. "Review: Heartbreak Tango." New York
Times (Dec. 16, 1973), pp. 14-15.
Hazaro, Lidia. "Narrative Techniques in Manuel Puig."
Latin American Literary Review (Fall-Winter 1973).
Puig, Manuel. "Growing Up at the Movies: A Chronology."
Review '72 No. 4-5 (1971-72), pp. 49-51.
Sarris, Andrew. "Rerunning Puig and Cabrera Infante."
Review '73 No. 9 (1973), pp. 46-48.

Chapter Nine - Severo Sarduy

Translations

Sarduy, Severo. "From Cuba with a Song," in Triple Cross:
Three Short Novels. Tr. Suzanne Jill Levine. New York:
Dutton, 1972.
_____. Cobra. Tr. and Preface by Suzanne Jill Levine.
New York: Dutton, 1975.

Selected Studies on Sarduy

Articles

Christ, Ronald. "Emergency Essay." Review '72 No. 6
(1972), pp. 33-36.
_____. "The New Latin American Novel." Partisan Re-
view Vol. 42 (1975), pp. 459-463.
Cixous, Hélène. "A Text Twister." Review '74 No. 13
(1974), pp. 26-31.
González-Echeverría, Roberto. "Interview: Severo Sarduy."
Diacritics Vol. 2, No. 3 (1972), pp. 41-45.
_____. "Rehearsal for Cobra." Review '74 No. 13
(1974), pp. 38-44.
Johndraw, Donald R. "Total Reality in Sarduy's Search for
lo cubano." Romance Notes Vol. 13 (1972), pp. 445-452.
Levine, Suzanne Jill. "Discourse as Bricolage." Review
'74 No. 13 (1974), pp. 32-37.
_____. "J. L. Borges and S. Sarduy: Two Writers of

the Neo-Baroque." Latin American Literary Review
Vol. 2, No. 4 (1974), pp. 25-37.
_____. "Writing as Translation: Three Trapped Tigers
and a Cobra." Modern Language Notes Vol. 90 (1975),
pp. 265-277.
Monegal, Emir Rodríguez. "Metamorphosis of the Text."
Review '74 No. 13 (1974), pp. 16-22.
Sollers, Phillipe. "La boca obra." Review '74 No. 13
(1974), pp. 13-15.

Chapter Ten - José Donoso

Translations

Donoso, José. Coronation. Tr. Jocasta Goodwin. New
York: Knopf, 1965.
_____. This Sunday. Tr. Lorraine O'Grady Freeman.
New York: Knopf, 1967.
_____. Hell Has No Limits, in Triple Cross. Tr.
Suzanne Jill Levine and Hallie Taylor. New York: Dut-
ton, 1972.
_____. The Obscene Bird of Night. Tr. Hardie St.
Martin and Leonard Mades. New York: Knopf, 1973.
_____. The Boom in Spanish American Literature: A
Personal History. Tr. Gregory Kolovakos. New York:
Columbia University Press in association with the Center
for Inter-American Relations, 1977.
_____. The Charleston and Other Stories. Tr. Andrée
Conrad. Boston: Godine, 1977.
_____. Sacred Families. Tr. Andrée Conrad. New
York: Knopf, 1977.

Selected Criticism on Donoso

Books

McMurray, George R. José Donoso. Boston: Twayne
Pubs., 1979.

Articles

Center for Inter-American Relations. Review '73 No. 9,
Focus: José Donoso and The Obscene Bird of Night.
(1973).
Gertel, Zunilda. "Metamorphosis as a Metaphor of the

World. " Review '73 No. 9 (1973), pp. 20-23.
Hasset, John J. "The Obscure Bird of Night. " Review '73
    No. 9 (1973), pp. 27-30.
Monegal, Emir Rodríguez. "The Novel as Happening: An
    Interview with José Donoso. " Review '73 No. 9 (1973),
    pp. 34-39.

Conclusion

Books

Guibert, Rita. Seven Voices. New York: Vintage, 1972.
Harss, L. , and B. Dohmann. Into the Mainstream. New
    York: Harper, 1967.
Menton, Seymour. Prose Fiction of the Cuban Revolution.
    Austin: University of Texas Press, 1975.

Articles

Books Abroad Vol. 44, No. 1 (1970). Entire Winter issue
    devoted to "The Latin American Novel. "
Mead, Robert G. "After the Boom. " Americas Vol. 30,
    No. 4 (April 4, 1978), pp. 2-8.
Monegal, Emir Rodríguez. "Latin American Literature, "
    in World Literature Since 1945 (New York: Ungar, 1973),
    pp. 416-448.

APPENDIX

A. Alphabetical Listing of Authors and Works Treated in Depth

1. Cabrera Infante, Guillermo. View of Dawn in the Tropics (1978).

2. Carpentier, Alejo. Explosion in a Cathedral (1962).

3. Cortázar, Julio. A Manual for Manuel (1978).

4. Donoso, José. Sacred Families (1977).

5. Fuentes, Carlos. The Hydra Head (1978).

6. García Márquez, Gabriel. The Autumn of the Patriarch (1976).

7. Lezama Lima, José. Paradiso (1974).

8. Puig, Manuel. Kiss of the Spiderwoman (1979).

9. Sarduy, Severo. Cobra (1975).

10. Vargas Llosa, Mario. Captain Pantoja and the Special Service (1978).

B. Listing of Reviews of Novels in American Publications

1. Cabrera Infante, Guillermo. View of Dawn in the Tropics.

142

Bookworld v. 75, Jan. 28, 1979, p. 4.
National Review v. 31, March 30, 1979, p. 434.
Kenyon Review v. 46, April 15, 1978, p. 888.
Library Journal v. 103, Sept. 15, 1978, p. 1765.
Nation v. 227, Nov. 4, 1978, p. 477.
Publishers Weekly v. 214, Oct. 9, 1978, p. 64.

2. Carpentier, Alejo. Explosion in a Cathedral.

America v. 109, Nov. 23, 1963, p. 682.
Best Sellers v. 23, Aug. 1, 1963, p. 149.
Library Journal v. 88, Aug. 7, 1963, p. 2925.
New Statesman v. 65, March 22, 1963, p. 430.
New York Herald Tribune, Aug. 4, 1963, p. 1.
New York Times, July 28, 1963, p. 4.

3. Cortázar, Julio. A Manual for Manuel.

Choice v. 15, January 1979, p. 1524.
Christian Science Monitor, Dec. 4, 1978, p. B4.
Library Journal v. 103, Nov. 1, 1978, p. 2261.
New York Review of Books v. 25, Oct. 12, 1978, p. 61.
New York Times, Nov. 19, 1978, p. 30.
New Republic v. 179, Oct. 21, 1978, p. 41.

4. Donoso, José. Sacred Families.

Atlantic v. 240, September 1977, p. 96.
Choice v. 14, November 1977, p. 1220.
Library Journal v. 102, Aug. 15, 1977, p. 1675.
New York Times, June 26, 1977, p. 14.
Saturday Review v. 4, July 9, 1977, p. 30.
Time v. 109, June 27, 1977, p. 68.

5. Fuentes, Carlos. The Hydra Head.

Library Journal v. 103, Dec. 15, 1978, p. 2536.
New Republic v. 179, Dec. 23, 1978, p. 39.
New Statesman v. 97, Mar. 9, 1979, p. 334.
New York Times, Jan. 2, 1979, p. 4.
Publishers Weekly v. 214, Nov. 13, 1978, p. 53.
Spectator v. 242, Mar. 10, 1979.

6. García Márquez, Gabriel. The Autumn of the Patriarch.

Atlantic v. 238, December 1976, p. 115.
Choice v. 13, Fall 1977, p. 1604.

Library Journal v. 101, Nov. 15, 1976, p. 2394.
New York Review of Books v. 23, Dec. 9, 1976, p. 57.
New York Times, Oct. 31, 1976, p. 1.
Saturday Review v. 4, Dec. 11, 1976, p. 68.

7.   Lezama Lima, José.   Paradiso.

Choice v. 11, July-August 1974, p. 767.
Library Journal v. 99, April 1, 1974, p. 1058.
Nation v. 218, May 11, 1974, p. 600.
New Republic v. 170, June 15, 1974, p. 27.
New York Review of Books v. 21, April 18, 1974, p. 14.
New York Times, April 21, 1974, p. 27.

8.   Puig, Manuel.   Kiss of the Spiderwoman.

Kirkus Review v. 47, Feb. 1, 1979, p. 150.
Publishers Weekly v. 215, Feb. 12, 1979, p. 118.
New York Times, April 23, 1979, p. 17.

9.   Sarduy, Severo.   Cobra.

Christian Science Monitor, April 9, 1975, p. 27.
Library Journal v. 99, Nov. 15, 1974, p. 2983.
New York Review of Books v. 22, March 27, 1975,
     p. 27.
New York Times, March 9, 1975, p. 18.
New Yorker v. 50, January 27, 1975, p. 102.

10.   Vargas Llosa, Mario.   Captain Pantoja and the Special
Service.

Library Journal v. 103, Feb. 1, 1978, p. 387.
New York Times, April 9, 1978, p. 11.
National Review v. 30, July 7, 1978, p. 852.
Nation v. 226, April 1, 1978, p. 377.
New Republic v. 178, May 20, 1978, p. 36.
New Statesman v. 96, Oct. 20, 1978, p. 519.

INDEX

All major novels discussed in this book are listed under their English title. Underlined page numbers indicate location of most extensive information. Titles are followed by author's name in parentheses.

145